GW00739283

TWO YEARS AND
AN
EARLY BREAKFAST

By the same Author:

We Will Remember Them
Peacehaven's Old Tin School

ABOUT THE AUTHOR

Malcolm Troak was born and bred in
Sussex and can therefore claim to be
one of the 'Men from Sussex.'
Educated at Clarks College Brighton
he spent his National Service years
with the Royal Sussex Regiment.
A Company Director with the Parker
Pen Company, he retired in 1993.
Malcolm has always had a very keen
and active interest in both local and
Military History.
He and Wife still live in East Sussex
as do his three children and seven
grandchildren.

TWO YEARS
AND
AN EARLY BREAKFAST

Dedicated to all who served as
national servicemen

By

Malcolm Troak

New Anzac Publications

Published By:
New Anzac Publications
30 Central Avenue
Telscombe Cliffs
East Sussex BN10 7LY

© Copyright 2003
Malcolm Troak

The right of Malcolm Troak to be identified as the author of
this work has been asserted by him in accordance with the
Copyright, Designs and Patents Act 1988.

All Rights Reserved
No reproduction, copy or transmission of this publication
may be made without written permission.
No paragraph of this publication may be reproduced,
copied or transmitted save with the written permission or in accordance
with the provisions of the Copyright Act 1956 (as amended).
Any person who does any unauthorised act in relation to
this publication may be liable to criminal
prosecution and civil claims for damage.

First published in 2003

ISBN: 0 9539115 2 7

Printed by:
ProPrint
Riverside Cottages
Old Great North Road
Stibbington
Cambs. PE8 6LR

CONTENTS

Back Cover Picture
     Gun Cleaning Suez 1951
     Molyneux, Stevens, Mills, Gurr, Boiling
     Troak, Filsell and Ayling

FOREWORD

Between 1945 and 1962 the majority of our soldiers were National Servicemen. For Britain's colonial Empire and overseas interests, they held the ring. These young men faced down and outfought North Korean and Chinese regulars, and terrorists of every complexion in Malaya, Cyprus, Kenya and Suez. One wonders if their achievements have ever been properly recognised; and they did it all under conditions of meagre pay and often very basic accommodation and amenities; and for many of them their service was compulsorily extended from 18 months to 2 years in order to meet Britains overseas and cold war commitments. Perhaps the officers and NCO's who trained them, in a few short weeks, to meet these challenges should also allow themselves a gentle pat on the back.

Malcolm Troak gives us a light-hearted but dead accurate account of the life of a National Serviceman in the Royal Sussex Regiment during the Suez troubles, and in the UK including the Coronation parade and the Freedom Marches through Sussex towns. It will bring back many memories, and smiles to the lips, of those who shared his 'Two Years and an Early Breakfast'. Two of his comments catch the imagination in particular. First, the ex-Royal Sussex ticket collector at Brighton station, who would have given Mr Troak the complete Regimental history had there not been a long queue at the barrier! and second, his comment that during training at Chichester there was none of the bullying one has sometimes read about recently . . . 'Our NCO's were tough but they did adopt quite a fatherly attitude to us raw recruits' . . . and he suggests that this was because they all belonged to the same Regimental family. This must be true; those who would rationalise training for reasons of economy should not ignore the strengths of Britain's regimental system. This spirit lives on; there are still, in 2003, some 500 members of the Royal Sussex Regimental Association, with nine branches throughout Sussex and in London.

Mr Troak talks of the 'icing on the cake' in his last paragraph. As this goes to print we have just heard that after many years of campaigning, the MOD has at last agreed to recommend to

Her Majesty that those who secured Britain's position in the Canal Zone and thereby brought the Egyptian government to the negotiating table, should be awarded the General Service Medal. This is thoroughly deserved.

Finally with a note of regret, this Foreword could not be written by John Stephenson who was Malcolm Troak's Platoon Commander. He very sadly died after a short illness on the 50th Anniversary of his carrying the Royal Sussex Regimental Colour on the 1953 Coronation Parade.

Robin McNish
Funtington,
Chichester.

INTRODUCTION

What prompted me to write a book on something which happened over fifty years ago?

The simple answer - grandchildren.

Two of my grandsons were studying the effects of the Second World War as one of their subjects for their Spring Term curriculum. They both came around to see me and asked, 'What did you do in the War, Grandad?'

When I explained that I hadn't served during the War they both said 'But you were in the Army because we have all seen your photos.'

It was then I had to start explaining about National Service, and about my two years conscription.

They were obviously fascinated when I spoke about guns, tanks, Egypt, two years away from home and how I had felt at that time. The more I got into the subject the more I realised how much real detail I could still remember, almost as though it were yesterday, people, names, places, good times, bad times. etc.

Although only two years in my lifetime it had quite obviously created an impact which I could recall with ease.

Having satisfied my grandsons' natural curiosity, I thought about putting pen to paper and recording for future generations the story of my two years National Service.

The time was also pertinent because in July 2003 I would have been demobbed fifty years - almost a lifetime!

So this is how the book happened!

During my initial research I could find very little written about National Service available in the libraries. Probably six books at the most of any real significance, which is quite surprising when one considers that non war time National Service ran from 1945 with the last conscripts being demobbed in 1963 a total of eighteen years.

During this time National Service was either enjoyed or endured by over two million young Britons.

Although written in chronological order I have attempted to present something which is not a diary of events but the day to day true stories of a young National Service Infantry man in the early 1950's. Good times, bad times, warts and all encapsulated in two years and an early breakfast.

Malcolm Troak

ACKNOWLEDGEMENTS

It never ceases to amaze me how supportive and encouraging people can be when one first mentions the idea of writing and publishing a book.

So many individuals came forward with ideas and suggestions as to how to present this book, that all I can say is thank you very much to you all.

However I would like to thank specifically the following:-

Alan Readman, West Sussex Record Office, Peacehaven Library, Brighton Family Record Centre, The Royal Sussex Regimental Association, Ashley Price (APA Secretarial), Bob Welsh (WASP), my grandchildren for putting the idea of this book into my head, all my old 'muckers' from 51/14 Group who really made this book possible. Colonel Robin McNish who so kindly at very short notice agreed to read my draft manuscript and write the foreword to this book, and last but not least all of my family for their continuous support during the long hours of research and writing when perhaps I should have been cutting the grass!

**'QUARTER BLOWN AND NOTHING READY,
BUT I'LL BE THERE AT MARKER STEADY'**

1

HOW IT ALL BEGAN

I suppose my National Service really started on May 16 1951, my eighteenth birthday.

That was the date on which, under the law of the land operating at that time, I was instructed to 'Register' at my local branch of the Ministry of Labour and National Service. This edict applied to all males upon reaching their 18th birthday.

At the time I was working at CVA Jigs Moulds and Tools in Coombe Road, Brighton as a Student Engineer. I was a late starter in industry having stayed on at Clarks College to sit for the Oxford School Certificate, hence Student Engineer.

As a student it may have been possible for me to request a deferment from National Service until my trade training was complete. However, I decided to 'Bite the Bullet' and get my two years National Service out of the way.

After 'registering' events took off very quickly. Within two weeks, the end of May, I was directed to attend a medical and assessment session at Oddfellow's Hall on the Corner of Queen's Road and North Road Brighton.

Oddfellows Hall, Brighton.
Many hundreds of National Servicemen passed through these doors to receive a pre-military medical examination.

Oddfellows Hall, long since demolished and replaced by insurance offices, had been used for many years as the local military medical assessment centre. It was a most austere and unwelcoming early Victorian building, very dark and draughty.

The medical examination was to enable the Doctors to assess and place you in one of three categories. A1 was the top category and meant the person was fit to be placed in any military unit and was an absolute minimum for the infantry. There was a fourth grade which meant the person was medically unfit and therefore not fit for military service. Records show that 15% of all annual intakes fell into this category.

I remember speaking to a local lad during a break in proceedings, who wanted to emulate his father and join the Parachute Regiment. Unfortunately, he had lost an eye in an air rifle accident. However, he had passed the eye test by memorising the Eye Test chart so that when the Doctor covered his good eye he would be able to 'read' down to the bottom line! I often wonder how far he got in entering his chosen regiment.

The medical assessment was very basic - specimen, bend over, cough, can you hear me when I whisper? Read that wall chart, have you had any of the following illnesses, etc. etc?

An aptitude test then followed the medical. In my case this consisted of disassembling a standard house lock and putting it back together again in a certain amount of time. Several of the 'non mechanised' types got into a terrible mess with springs flying all over the place!

The next thing was a written test, simple sums and some writing, all very basic. At the same time we had to fill in a questionnaire indicating which branch of the service we would like to be considered for and why.

I asked to be considered for the Royal Electrical and Mechanical Engineers (REME) because of my engineering training, as did several of the people I spoke to.

Eventually my National Service Medical Grade Card arrived, it announced that I had been graded A1, so at least I was considered by the army to be fit!

All I now needed was to receive my enlistment documentation instructing me when and where to report and more important, which Regiment or Corps.

Called To The Colours

In mid June 1951 a buff coloured envelope dropped through the letter box - it was my Military Enlistment papers. The day of reckoning had arrived!

I was instructed to report to Chichester Barracks, Depot of the Royal Sussex Regiment on Thursday 26th July 1951. So it was to be the Infantry!

The enlistment notice included a Railway Warrant to Chichester plus other detailed information regarding what to take in the way of personal items, ration books and coupons etc. It also gave a reminder to inform my employer who was required by law to keep your job open and to take you back after National Service.

The 'Big Day' was always on a Thursday. The army had two drafts a month. My draft number was 51-14 which was the 14th draft in 1951. Draft numbers were a very good way of establishing how much service a soldier had got in, and was much used in the Barrack Room banter, ie 'get some in'!

So I had approximately six weeks to 'get my house in order' and prepare for the next two years.

YOU'RE IN THE ARMY NOW

Thursday 26th July 1951, enlistment day, and what a wonderful summer's day it was. Even after all these years I can remember it as clearly as though it were yesterday.

At Brighton Station the ticket collector on the Portsmouth platform said 'Going to Chi. I see, Royal Sussex I expect.'

'Yes,' I replied. 'Two years National Service.'

'Lovely family regiment, the Orange Lilies, the old 35th of Foot, you know. Best cap badge in the British Army. I enjoyed my service with them, I wish I was going with you,' he said.

Without doubt, if there had not been other passengers waiting to have their tickets punched, he would have given me the whole Regimental history!

As I passed along the platform I heard him shout 'And I still cry my eyes out when we sing Sussex By the Sea at the annual reunion at the Dome.'

After a short journey along the west coast the train arrived at Chichester railway station. Several other lads of the same age group as myself got off, all with various types of hand luggage.

Outside were parked two army lorries - one knowledgeable guy described them as 'three tonners'.

Nearby was a very smart Sergeant complete with bright red sash and a clipboard in his hand.

'Any conscripts for the Barracks?' he shouted. 'Come over here and have your name checked off.'

Once we were checked in it was in the back of the three tonners and a short ride through the city to the Barracks. There were around a dozen 'conscripts' in the same lorry as me, all of them the usual eighteen year old mix; quiet, noisy, long haired, short haired, etc. I recognised two who had got on the train at Brighton and who I subsequently got to know very well, Tony Blunt from Brighton and Curly Fuller from Lewes.

After about ten minutes we were turning into the Barracks on the north side of the city. There were two very smart looking Corporals who came across, undid the tailboard and told us to jump out. We were told to line up, answer our names again and then follow them into the special orderly room.

The
Depot

THE ROYAL SUSSEX
REGIMENT.

CHICHESTER.

Inside were lines of trestle tables with uniformed clerks behind. As our name was called we had to go to the relevant desk. Surprisingly I remember we were supplied with a chair on which we could sit during the interview.

Imagine my surprise to find that the clerk interviewing me was none other than Michael Larter from Peacehaven, a fellow I used to box with. He told me he had been with the Royal Sussex around six months.

I was then issued with my army number 22508130 which even after fifty years I have no problem in remembering. Also my AB64 Part I, which was to all intents and purposes like a passport. I was told to carry it with me at all times and never, never lose it. There was a further Service Book, AB 64 Part II, which was to be my pay book. All my ration cards and coupons were then surrendered. Rationing, a left over from the Second World War, did not completely end until July 1954.

I remember asking Michael how many conscripts would be in the 51-14 draft. He told me that it was a very large draft of over eighty, and was in order to bring the 1st Battalion in Egypt up to strength. Apparently there had been a few problems in the Canal Zone and more trouble was expected. I, for one, was completely unaware of the Suez problems, in fact I didn't even know that the Royal Sussex were serving in Egypt. The Newspapers in 1951 were obviously full of the conflicts in Korea and Malaya but nothing on Egypt.

He also told me to expect six weeks 'square bashing' at Chichester then a further four weeks advanced training at, probably, Canterbury in Kent.

So it looked like an overseas posting to Egypt with an Infantry Regiment.

Having taken care of all the documentation we were then told we would be allocated a 'bed space' in the main Barracks, in the newly renovated Sandhurst Block. I was taken upstairs by a young soldier called 'Dickie' Bird, who told me he had been back-squadded due to illness and that he would be joining the 51-14 squad. He was a mine of information telling me amongst other things that all civilian clothes would have to be sent home. The only item which could be retained would be sensible shoes, not 'Brothel Creepers' or suedes!

I was immensely impressed with the Barracks. Everything of course was spotless and the wooden flooring absolutely gleaming. We each had one metal bed, mattress and steel wardrobe.

Dickie told me the wooden floor had to be bumped (polished) every day and treated with great care. It looked like hard work to me!

Apparently, we were only the second National Service draft to be trained at Chichester as previously all training had been done at Shorncliffe, up on the cliffs near Dover.

We even had indoor toilets, washrooms with hot and cold running water which apparently was the height of luxury in the army! (The army called these areas 'Ablutions'). It hadn't always been like this. The Barracks had originally been built in 1803 to accommodate French prisoners of war. Remnants of wooden framed Peninsula Blocks were still in evidence in 1951, and they certainly looked very basic indeed.

Kitting Out

I always thought this part of the proceedings would have made a good skit for a comedy show! We were lined up and then 'marched' off to the Quartermaster's Stores (Q M Stores). Inside was this long line of trestle tables behind which was a multitude of depot staff and behind them were huge racks of military clothing and equipment. There was one Warrant Officer in charge, presumably the Regimental Quarter Master Sergeant (RQMS).

The procedure was that the new recruit started at one end and was handed over items of kit at each station. But what sizes for the uniforms etc? This is where the QM came into his own. He would look at each recruit, mentally sizing him up, and then bellow out something almost like a foreign language to his line of servers. This would be the size of uniform, etc., which would be supplied. It was also a new language. For some reason the army would use words in reverse order, ie badge-cap, drawers-cellular, bag-kit, etc.

The range of clothing and equipment was bewildering. Great Coat, two Battledresses, set of Denims, two pairs of boots each with the regulation set of 13 studs per boot. Mess tins, masses of webbing, helmet steel, etc. etc. At the end of the line it was a problem, either to see over the kit held in both arms or indeed to hold on to it. To drop anything and disturb the proceeding was a fate worse than death!

We had to transport the mass of clothing and equipment back to our barrack room and await instructions.

TRAINING AT CHICHESTER

The whole draft had been split into two Platoons - Gibraltar and Alamein, with approximately forty in each platoon. There were two Corporals to each platoon with a Sergeant responsible overall for all training.

I was put in Alamein platoon under the control of Corporal Coxall, who came from Littlehampton, and Corporal Joe Vine, who came from Eastbourne. My understanding was that both Corporals were National Service Men.

A few members of 51-14 group at Chichester with the training NCO's. On the left Cpl. Coxall, in the centre Sgt. (Pawnee) Waters, and far right Cpl. Joe Vine.

The first thing we were taught was how to make a bed army style, an exercise we had to carry out every single morning. (It was quite apparent that, like myself, most of the platoon had never made a bed before!)

We had been issued with five blankets and two sheets. One blanket had to be tightly spread over the mattress and each of the four corners neatly folded in 'Hospital' style. Three blankets were then folded in a regulation way to a regulation size then placed blanket, sheet, blanket, sheet, blanket. The last blanket was then wrapped around the sheets and blankets. All edges had to be square and levelled off. This bed making method was carried out throughout my two years service.

We were then instructed in the delights of blancoing all our webbing, how to clean brasses and last of all how to 'bull' our two pairs of brand new army boots. What a nightmare!

Blanco is a block of chalky substance, in our case khaki in colour. Using a wet Blanco brush the top of the block is made into a paste. This paste must be neither too wet or too dry. With the aid of the brush each piece of webbing, there were probably twenty separate items, had Blanco applied to it. Once mastered the method was quite straight forward but it took a great deal of practice.

The other 'nice' thing about the webbing was that it all had brass buckles and cleats attached. They all had to be polished with the proverbial yellow duster and the inimitable Brasso. All brasses had to be cleaned front, back and inside. Absolutely no Brasso was allowed on the parts blancoed. It was a nightmare to start with but fortunately in our squad we had a couple of recruits who had spent many years in the army cadets and had fully mastered the art of cleaning equipment. They were, without exception, very happy to pass on their knowledge.

'Boots, ammunition for the use of', two brand new pairs which were manufactured with all those little pimples over them which had to be 'ironed' out with the heated handle of a spoon. Once they had been 'ironed' smooth the job of generating a super gloss finish could begin.

The best black polish was apparently Kiwi, which we had to obtain from the NAAFI. It was then a yellow duster and plenty of 'spit and polish' and hours and hours of little circles with polish and duster. The heels and toe caps of the boots had to shine as though they had been French polished.

We had to select a 'best pair of boots' which were only used for Ceremonial parades and for placing on our beds for kit inspections. 'Best Boots' were a prized possession and were treated with kid gloves.

The worst thing which could happen was to have to send them to the Regimental Boot Repairer for repair. They would be collected in large Hessian sacks with many other boots, repaired and returned. What a sorry state they would be when delivered back to the owner; all scuffed and battered and in need of complete re-polishing.

Berets

Before joining the Army, berets always appeared to be a very simple form of headdress, I soon found out they were not!

The first thing we had to do was to tuck in the two ends of the ribbon at the back of the beret so that they were completely hidden from sight. As Corporal Coxall said 'We don't want you looking like some of those Continentals!'

The two berets as issued were like floppy pancakes. We had to each beat, soak and cajole the beret so that it could be placed directly on the head in one movement; fitting the head precisely. The leather band had to be parallel and exactly one and half inches above the eye. It had to be brushed every time you wore it so that no flick, hairs or other debris was visible.

When 'fitted' properly the beret indicated a soldier rather than a recruit. Again we had to select a best and second best beret.

Once we had all our kit assembled we were instructed that everything had to be individually marked with our eight digit number, before the next morning. What a nightmare this turned out to be, an operation which in some cases went on until the early hours of the morning. Metal items had to be stamped. There was one set of stamps and one hammer between forty recruits! 'Hurry up and finish!' Clothes and webbing had to be marked by using wooden stamps (they looked as though they had originated in Caxton's day) and an indelible ink pad. Again one set of wooden stamps between forty recruits! It was, I remember, a pretty sleepless night! Fortunately we really did have a great bunch in our group. The majority were from the Sussex area with a sprinkling from the Kent borders.

Certainly the ones who had deferred their National Service such as Fred Wingfield, who was twenty one, conveyed a 'fatherly' approach to lads who struggled with bringing their kit up to standard.

The 'Real' training begins

We had been told that training would consist of learning to march, foot and arms drill, use of the .303 Lee Enfield rifle, Bren and Sten gun. At each stage we would be tested and marked accordingly. These tests in typical army fashion were called TOETS (Tests of Elementary Training). Results were included in the AB64 Pt 1 for posterity!

We would also be tested for physical fitness, failure to meet the standard could mean back squadding we were warned.

Regimental history would be 'drummed' into us, and again we would be tested, ie. When was the Regiment formed? 1701 Sir, What is the meaning of the motto Honi Soit Qui Mal y Pense? etc.

There would also be a very competitive edge introduced by way of the two platoons Alamein and Gibraltar. We were assured that each of the training Corporals was 'very keen' to have their platoon on top of the league - most ominous!

During the next three weeks our feet did not touch the ground. We were harried from six in the morning till very late at night. One of the more 'memorable' pleasures was being given three minutes to get upstairs and change from battle dress into PT (Physical Training) kit and leave each bed space at inspection level. It really was mayhem.

Another fond memory is of eighty recruits running through the centre of Chichester dressed in Army boots, black PT shorts and red PT vest. You can only imagine the noise of thirteen steel studs per foot pounding down on the City cobbles.

After three weeks when we could prove that we were capable of wearing a beret correctly, that we could polish our brasses, that we did have razor sharp creases in our battle dress, we were allowed out. This is easier than it sounds. Before going out of the Barracks we had to report to the Guard Room where the Regimental Police were housed.

Outside was a very tall polished mirror. We had to stand in front of this, check our dress and then be inspected by one of the Regimental Police. If you passed muster you were allowed out until I believe 10pm. Anyone caught improperly dressed was sent back to the barracks at the double.

The Firing Ranges

After four weeks intense training we were informed that we would be going to the ranges at Kithurst, near Storrington to fire live rounds with the .303 Lee Enfield, the Bren and the Sten guns. Some of the 'old sweats' kindly told us that the .303 had a kick like a mule and that we would come back with black and blue shoulders!

On the morning of the Ranges we were introduced to the delights of the Army haversack rations. Each soldier collected his rations from the cookhouse which consisted of two sandwiches - each slice of bread approximately five inches square and half an inch thick. They would normally be filled with some form of meat or paste. Filling they were, but tasty, definitely not.

We were driven to the Kithurst ranges in the back of the three ton Bedford lorries carrying our rifles with us.

The actual range was at the bottom of Kithurst Hill a most lonely and deserted area - probably the reason it was chosen. The Butts which were immediately at the base of the hill was simply a long trench dug into the chalk, with a chalk parapet.

Six foot high targets were mounted on lifting frames in order to mark and then paste up the bullet holes. It was hard work in the Butts, and you were frequently showered with chalk if someone was off target.

Before we commenced shooting the officer in charge instructed us to 'Empty your bladders, it is impossible to shoot accurately on a full bladder!'

I thoroughly enjoyed the shoot and at the end of the day was classified as a first class shot. This was useful in the future as once a year the whole Regiment has to shoot in order to establish classification. The better the classification the better the pay and vice versa!

At the end of the shoot we were all lined up and told in no uncertain terms that to take live or empty rounds off the Range was a punishable offence and could result in a Court Martial. Before leaving the ranges therefore we had to declare to the officer in charge 'No live rounds or empty cases sir.' This was repeated every time I shot during my two years National Service.

After a particularly tiring but interesting day, we returned to Barracks, but we were not finished. We had to 'boil out' our rifles. Behind the cookhouse were metal vats which were full of scalding water. Having removed the bolt from our rifle we had to fill an enamel jug with this scalding water and pour it down the barrel. Apparently this prevented the barrel from sweating after shooting and rusting up (a rusty barrel was a punishable offence). Today's Health and Safety executive would certainly not have approved of this practice!

Passing Out

The passing out parade was the culmination of our six weeks training. In the final few days before the parade we were drilled by Sergeant Waters. A short man, very smart, with a bristling moustache and a really gravely voice (he sounded as though he gargled with gravel). For hours on end we rehearsed our foot and arms drill until surprisingly enough the whole eighty of us were moving as one. 'Just get it like that on the day and even I will be happy,' he roared. Actually his bark was worse than his bite. His nickname was 'Pawnee' presumably something to do with Waters, but we never called him this in earshot!

Our passing out parade took place on the main square of the Barracks on Wednesday 5th September 1951, almost six weeks to the day since we had passed through the Barrack gates.

A typical passing out parade at The Depot,
The Royal Sussex Regt. Chichester.

The inspecting officer was Colonel Parry who commanded the Home Counties Brigade - needless to say a very high ranking officer. Fortunately the whole parade went off without a hitch, nobody fainted or dropped their rifle, and the drill was immaculate.

Awards were made to the best recruit from each platoon, Fred Wingfield won it for Gibraltar and Bert Gurr for Alamein.

Parents and wives had been invited to the parade and also to tea in the NAAFI afterwards. When everyone had departed we all celebrated in great style, having survived our first six weeks in the Army.

Next day we were going to have some well earned leave. However, not before we had received our TAB Booster jab. This is really a horrible jab which can lead to twenty four hour fever and a very painful arm. We all had to line up in the main cookhouse with arms bared. A medical orderly wiped the top of the arm with some form of antiseptic and the Medical Officer applied the jab.

Unlike today, a new needle wasn't used every time. Oh no, the MO had a beautiful chrome and glass syringe which he continually refilled from a tube of vaccine. When he thought the needle was getting blunt he might think about changing it! I also remember a couple of guys 'passing out' before they had even had their jab!

So it was home on leave with a very painful arm!

I have often been asked if I experienced any bullying or sadistic instructors during my initial six weeks training. The answer is a positive no.

I did anticipate that we would experience some because of horror stories from friends of mine who had done their initial training with some of the larger Corps. With these there was a real mix of soldiers from all over the country, without any of the affiliation to say a County infantry regiment. Our NCO's were tough but they did adopt quite a fatherly attitude towards us as raw recruits.

Perhaps this was because they wore the same regimental Cap badge and knew we were destined to serve with the First Battalion, part of the same family.

WEMYSS BARRACKS - CANTERBURY

We now knew that when we returned from leave we would be going to Wemyss Barracks in the centre of Canterbury to complete our training.

This would consist of more advanced training on such things as the 2 inch Mortar, throwing the No 36 hand-grenade, field craft and more advanced drill.

Wemyss Barracks was the training centre for the Home Counties brigade, regiments such as the Royal West Kents, Royal Sussex and the Buffs.

Back at Chichester after our well earned leave it was time to pack up all our gear ready for transportation to Canterbury.

One thing we had to learn was how to pack a kit bag. The art was to roll the kit bag down to the bottom. Start by placing boots and other items to form the base. All other items of clothes are then 'rolled' and placed to the sides of the kit bag. The sides are progressively pulled up until the bag is full. In this way when unpacked all kit can be removed almost crease free.

We were transported to Canterbury by train again having been issued with the ubiquitous haversack rations!

Having detrained at Canterbury we had to form up and march to the Barracks as a unit.

One incident which sticks vividly in my mind is having to stop at a set of traffic lights. We were marching along very smartly when we were suddenly ordered to halt; all eighty of us came to a blistering and noisy halt. The reason - the traffic lights had turned red and we of course had to abide by the rules of the road!

I can remember there were gasps of dismay when we finally arrived at Wemyss Barracks - our honeymoon was over. Wemyss had been built over two hundred years before our arrival - and had been a cavalry barracks for many years, you could almost smell the horses!

Sleeping quarters were either above the old stables or in corrugated iron huts. Once again our draft was split into two platoons. I was placed in 'S' Platoon 3 Company Home Counties

Brigade Depot and was allocated a bed space in one of the corrugated iron huts.

The floors were made of concrete slabs which seemed to generate dust and dirt and were certainly freezing cold in the morning.

There was a beautiful blackened tortoise cast iron stove in the middle of the hut. The buckets of coal looking absolutely polished - as they were.

We subsequently found out to our utter disgust that the stoves were never used during the week as they took too long to clean, and would fail morning inspection. Remember this was mid September and it was already turning cold.

The ablutions were also a far cry from those we had used in Chichester. At Wemyss they were well away from any sleeping quarters. The ones which our hut used had all the appearance of a corrugated iron cattle shed.

Dimly lit by a couple of 100 watt bulbs, a long metal trough went the length of the building. Above this were old fashioned taps suspended from iron pipes. From these taps it was possible to obtain a poor flow of very tepid water.

Personally to avoid all the last minute rushing I would wash and shave at 6am each morning. My goodness I can still remember how bitterly cold it was.

The other new experience at Wemyss was the bugle calls. Everything was carried out to a bugle call - from Reveille to lights out.

We soon learnt the meaning of each of the bugle calls and in my case particularly 'Retreat'.

Four of us were walking to the NAAFI after we had finished for the day. We heard this particular bugle call and openly discussed how we liked the tune and what was it.

Suddenly there was an almighty roar from a Company Sergeant Major standing to attention on the edge of the square.

'Stand still those four stupid soldiers.' We froze on the spot!

When the call was finished he gave us all a dressing down - didn't we recognise the Retreat? Didn't we know that every evening the Retreat was played and 'Everybody' but everybody stood still wherever they were, as a sign of respect to those who had died in action.

We all agreed we were stupid soldiers!

The emphasis on our next four weeks training was less on drill and more on weapon and field training.

S. Platoon.
No. 3 Company, H.C.B.D., Canterbury.

In charge of our platoon was a Sergeant from the Royal Sussex, whose name I forget, and a Corporal Barratt from the Buffs. Our platoon officer - a lieutenant also came from the Buffs.

A typical day's training programme would have looked like this.

06.00	Reveille
07.00	Breakfast
07.45	Clean room and lay out beds
08.15	Muster Parade
08.30 - 09.30	Foot & Arms Drill
09.30 - 10.00	Lecture
10.00 - 10.00	Lecture
10.00 - 10.30	NAAFI BREAK
10.30 - 11.00	Weapon training

11.00 - 12.00	Field craft
12.00 - 12.45	Physical training
12.45 - 13.45	Lunch
13.45 - 14.45	Military education
14.45 - 16.15	Miniature rifle range
17.30	Tea
22.30	Lights out

There were two other groups of soldiers who had a much tougher training regime than we did. One group was a large draft from the Royal West Kents. They were being trained for operations in Malaya. Their advanced training was for six weeks, against our four and much emphasis apparently was placed on physical fitness and field craft. They also used a shorter version of the Lee Enfield rifle as this had worked out better under jungle conditions.

We were all glad we were not going to Malaya!

The other group was PLs - Potential Leaders who hoped to go on to become Infantry Officers. They were recognisable by their white shoulder flashes and the pace of their training. They worked from morning until night continually pushed by their NCOs.

We in fact had 'lost' one of the members of our platoon at Chichester to become a PL. I remember him well. His name was Elliott, a member of the famous tool shop, Elliotts, in London Road, Brighton.

I knew he had studied at Brighton and Hove Grammar School and had been a very active member of their very strong Army Cadet force.

He did eventually arrive in Egypt as a Second Lieutenant.

One night I remember there was a real panic on. A young recruit, I believe he was in the East Surreys, had been shot in the stomach with a blank .303 cartridge. He eventually died of his wound.

Next day we were all paraded and warned of the dangers of firing blanks indiscriminately and certainly not at people.

Our Corporal demonstrated by firing a blank at a tin can and putting a hole in the side.

We had always assumed blanks to be innocuous but they certainly were not.

The firing ranges we used were down on the Coast at Hythe, on the wide pebble beaches. We used to travel down in the back of Bedford three tonners with our rifles and haversack rations.

One of the more interesting shoots was the Donkey Derby.

The normal six foot targets were replaced by eight foot targets, which looked large even at five hundred yards. We would load ten rounds. Fire two at the five hundred yard point. Double down to the four hundred yard point fire two rounds. This would go on until the two hundred yard point. Here we would fire two rounds from the kneeling position, fix bayonets and charge to the hundred yard point and fire the final two shots from the standing positions. Of course the eight foot targets appeared as large as the side of a bus.

Unfortunately running on shingle is the most energy sapping form of exercise any body could possibly devise.

We stood and attempted to hold our rifles sufficiently steady to get a reasonable couple of shots off. It was almost impossible!

Another part of our advanced training was the 'throwing' of three No 36 Mills Hand Grenades.

This was done at a place called Dibgate not far from Folkestone. We each had to 'arm' three grenades in a sandbag bunker, and ensure the 'pin' was fully in place.

An officer was sited in an observation post at high level overlooking the throwing bunker. When instructed by our Sergeant to enter the throwing area we did so with our three handgrenades.

On his instructions we removed a pin and threw the grenade at a target some ten yards away.

The 'Bad bit' was we had to remain standing until the officer said 'down' when we could duck down behind the sand bag parapet with a couple of seconds to spare!

A couple of the guys panicked with their first throw and hardly got it over the parapet. They were told to duck immediately!

The four weeks passed remarkably quickly and we were ready for our second passing out parade.

This time we would be marching to a military band. Unfortunately it was to be only a Fife and drum band which according to Corporal Barratt was notoriously difficult to pick up a beat.

We had one practice run with the band the day before passing out, and the first fifteen minutes was disastrous. Instructors were going berserk. However we did eventually manage to pick up the beat and march in step around the square.

The next day went off without a hitch and we were all declared to be 'Trained Soldiers'.

Trained soldiers! Outside our hut after the passing out parade, Canterbury 1951.

This allowed us the privilege of a forty eight hour pass which really was most welcome as we also received a travel warrant.

As most of us came from Sussex we would catch the steam train from Canterbury to Ore where we had to change for the Southern Electric trains to Brighton.

It was quite a pleasant journey across the Romney and Pevensey marshes although relatively slow with stops at most of the stations on the way.

Three of the stations were called Wye, Chilham and Chartham. We used to say Why Killem and Cartem to Canterbury.

Although we had completed our four weeks advanced training we had no details of how or when or even if we would be going to Egypt to join the First Battalion in Suez.

I for one never did really understand how instructions came down for our group's movements. It just seemed to happen.

In the event when we returned from leave we were joined by Corporal Ted Streeter who told us he would be travelling with us to Egypt to rejoin the Regiment. More than that he knew no more!

He did however 'kindly' inform us that we would be filling in the next three weeks on camp fatigues. Every morning we were formed into working parties to either deliver coal to the married quarters, clean the Barrack grounds, paint the fence posts and anything else that could be thought of to avoid us getting bored.

Hugh Weekes, one of the few in our draft who could drive got a lovely job of driving a one tonner on local deliveries. It was such a 'cushy' job that he decided to stay at Wemyss and not come to Egypt with us.

One of the best fatigues I had was up the hill to the Howe Barracks, Regimental Headquarters of the Buffs. It was like the Savoy Hotel in comparison to Wemyss. The NAAFI was really first class and was open for most of the day.

Nobody bothered us - we were supposed to be picking up paper. Unfortunately this little hideaway only lasted three days.

During the third week in October we were informed of our travel details to Egypt, which was a welcome relief as the weather had turned bitterly cold with frost on most mornings.

We would be travelling to the Hook of Holland and overland to Trieste. From Trieste it would be by troopship to Port Said.

This was known as the MEDLOC Route (Middle East Line of Communications).

We were entitled to one week's embarkation leave prior to departure and it would then be off on our travels.

2

AND SO TO EGYPT

Back to Wemyss after a very restful embarkation leave and it was all 'systems go'.

Kit bags had to be printed with details of our final destination and filled with all items not required on voyage. We would not see our kit bags until we reached Egypt, they would be left to the tender mercies of the baggage party.

It was now early November. Canterbury was still bitterly cold, and we were very pleased to set off for Liverpool Street Station and on to Harwich to embark on our ferry crossing to The Hook of Holland.

What was quite surprising was how few of our draft of eighty had ever been to London before. It was a real eye opener for many of them.

The train pulled into the dockside at Harwich and there waiting was the Empire Wansbeck for our overnight crossing to Holland.

There were soldiers everywhere, the majority returning to bases in Germany, blanco of every colour ranging from brilliant white to black for the Rifle Brigade was very much in evidence.

We had been warned that the crossing could sometimes be rough across the North Sea in the winter months.

Our crossing was no exception, although personally I had a very good night's sleep. It was only when I awoke and went for a shave that I realised how bad it must have been. All sinks and basins and decks were awash with vomit. There were ashen faced squaddies laid out everywhere all looking like death warmed up. It must have been really rough!

We docked at the Hook very early next morning and our group disembarked and were escorted to the largest transit camp I have ever seen. It was absolutely enormous and was jam packed with troops having breakfast and awaiting for their next means of transportation.

BY TRAIN - THE MEDLOC 'C' ROUTE

As our group was going by the MEDLOC 'C' route, we would be travelling by train on the next leg of our journey.

Everything was wonderfully organised by the Royal Engineers Movement Control people and before long we were informed that our particular train was ready, and what a train it turned out to be. A magnificent German steam engine hauling coaches from the German Dining Car Company.

One compartment was allocated to four people. The two bottom seats and the two top storage shelves turned into very comfortable sleeping bunks at night.

We were given meal tickets with specific dining times and were called to the dining car by white coated German waiters.

Three course meals almost silver service, it was the height of luxury and was like travelling on a Pullman train. We were all most impressed.

Before long we were passing through Eindhoven and the Philips electrical factory which appeared to go on for many miles. We all remarked how very clean and well kept Holland was, and particularly noticed Dutch women scrubbing their front door steps and the amount of people riding bikes.

Next morning we passed into Germany where the first large city we came to was Cologne. The railway track ran alongside the magnificent cathedral which amazingly was in very good condition considering that on either side of it there was extensive bomb damage. Remember this was just six years after the end of the Second World War, and reconstruction had only recently begun.

The train basically followed the River Rhine into the centre of Germany, again most interesting scenery.

There were no stops at night, whilst we slept in our very comfortable bunks the train continued its inexorable progress.

Early one morning we approached the border between Germany and Austria. Officials boarded the train once we slowly entered Austria and checked each of the compartments, and the occupants.

We were then shunted into a siding whilst an Austrian Railways engine was coupled on to the rear of the train. This was because we were about to enter very mountainous country. What a magnificent journey it was through the centre of Austria. One minute we were looking up at snow covered mountains and the next at deep ravines with tumbling waterfalls.

Thomas Cook could not have bettered the journey we were making.

Eventually we arrived at Villach on the Austrian/Italian borders and again went through the checking procedures. From Villach it seemed a very short journey until we arrived at the port of Trieste on the Adriatic. We were all sorry to leave the comforts of our train but we were looking forward with some anticipation to our next part of the journey - a sea voyage.

BY SEA - THE EMPIRE TEST

Our troopship the Empire Test was tied up alongside the main harbour in Trieste. I remember she had a yellow funnel and appeared to be quite small. Rumour had it that she was a converted coal barge! She was quite old having been built in 1922.

I have subsequently established that the Empire Test was 'broken up' in October 1952, just twelve months after our journey. It was probably a happy release for anybody still to travel by troopship.

We all filed up the gangplank and down into the very bowels of the ship. To our horror we were told that we would be sleeping in hammocks - after the Lord Major's Show!

We set sail that night having been allowed a few hours in Trieste after we had stored our kit and learnt the art of slinging a hammock.

Meal times were arranged by Mess Decks. Each mess had to collect its food from the Galley, and take it back to the mess for distribution. The food was absolutely awful. Lunch would consist of a billy can of potatoes and a greasy stew like concoction. Obviously we had been spoilt on our train journey!

One of the real problems we all found was washing and shaving. The water used in the washrooms was salt water pumped directly out of the sea. Although we had been issued with 'special' soap it was almost impossible to raise even a semblance of a lather.

On our second night we hit a violent storm. The ship tossed and rolled alarmingly. It was so bad that at times the twin screws were out of the water. Without resistance the screws caused violent vibrations throughout the ship, it was quite frightening.

Several of my mates had to be isolated because of violent sea sickness. The only ones who appeared happy were the Galley staff who had very little food to prepare.

We were not impressed with the Adriatic or the Empire Test.

Calmer weather did eventually come along and we were able to venture on deck. There was a 'wet' canteen which served mainly Blue Cross Beer from Malta but not much else.

The Mediterranean Sea when we did finally reach it was so much better than the Adriatic but of course meant we were nearing the end of the voyage.

We were due to dock at Port Said on November 16 which we did exactly on time.

Port Said was alive with all kinds of military personnel and naval craft and of course the ubiquitous Arab 'Bum Boats'.

As soon as we docked these little boats with a couple of locals on board would throw a line up the side of the ship. A squaddie would catch it, and the Arab would attach a small wicker basket to his end and send up some pretty tacky souvenirs. If you liked the offering then you would commence to barter until both sides were satisfied. All harmless fun and a little indoctrination into Egypt.

One aspect which was quite noticeable was that all military personnel were armed. Officers had pistols in holsters. Military police had sten guns and everybody else had rifles - shades of things to come!

3

HODGSON'S CAMP - SUEZ

Unknown to us 'raw' recruits one of the Royal Sussex Officers who had travelled the same route as us was the new Commanding Officer, Lieutenant Colonel J B Ashworth DSO. He had previously had command of the Regiment in 1946-57 and from those who knew he was described as a 'Real Gentleman'.

The journey to our new camp was approximately one hundred miles from Port Said and basically followed the route of the Suez Canal.

Although we were actually in Egypt the area was known as the Canal Zone, and there was a very large area of this which because of the troubles was classed as an exclusion zone.

The Treaty road on which we travelled to our final destination was fairly narrow and made up with Tarmac. Military vehicles were travelling up and down it the whole time all with an armed guard alongside the driver. We passed many tented camps all fully occupied with different Infantry and Parachute battalions, and of course lots and lots of sand.

We also passed a very large monument and statue halfway along the road which we could see was to commemorate Ferdinand de Lesseps, the builder of the Suez Canal, which opened in 1869.

We eventually arrived at Hodgson's Camp which was a mixture of tented accommodation and brick built administration buildings.

The Royal Sussex had moved into the Camp at Suez in August 1949 and apart from a five month spell at Aquaba in 1950, had remained there ever since.

Hodgsons Camp, Suez.

We were reunited with our kit bags and directed to a small tented area. This was separate from the other company lines, and was in effect a holding area until we were allocated to a specific company.

Hardly were we unpacked than we were called outside and marched off to the QM Stores.

The purpose of this visit was to issue each of us with a rifle and a bandolier of fifty rounds of .303 ammunition.

We were instructed to carry our rifles and ammunition at all times and to sleep with the rifle attached to our bodies by the rifle sling. Things looked pretty serious indeed.

The camp as a whole seemed very empty, this was apparently due to the fact that most of the rifle companies were outside guarding such installations as the water filtration plant, railway signal boxes, and other important military buildings.

Next morning we were paraded together and marched off for a briefing on what to expect and what was expected of us.

First of all the officer gave a brief description of the current troubles and the background of how they started.

'It would appear that the Egyptians wanted the British out of the Canal Zone. The British has refused to move because amongst other things the Suez Canal was a critical supply line, and also an Anglo Egyptian treaty had been signed in 1936. This was a twenty year treaty and was due to expire in 1956.

On the 15th October 1951 the Egyptians announced 'Abrogation Day', a day of rejoicing throughout the land, the British would be pushed out of the Canal Zone and Egypt would be for the Egyptians - or so they thought.

On the 16th October it was decided that because of the deteriorating situation that the married families should be moved from their accommodation in Suez and Tewfik and into Hodgson's Camp. He was pleased to say that the whole move had been completed in one day, a notable achievement.

Since that time the Battalion had been actively engaged on road blocks and increased guards not only around the camp lines but also at towns like Fayid.

How would this affect you new recruits? First of all the Battalion had lost its civilian labourers, cooks, gardeners, sanitary men and kitchen boys. The only civilians on camp were one Palestinian tailor and the Officers Mess cook, so probably more fatigues!

The NAAFI was almost defunct as the staff had gone. However the good news (probably) was that supplies of Blanco, Brasso and boot polish were virtually non existent!

He then went on to housekeeping. Our address would now be MELF 15 (Middle East Land Force). There was a distinct possibility that all outgoing mail could be censored, so be warned.

As we were in MELF we were entitled to a Land Overseas Allowance (LOA) which currently was 11/0 per week (55p).We would be paid in local currency which was Piastres, but get used to calling it AKKERS because no soldier worth his salt would talk about Piastres.

In the next couple of days he told us we would each be individually interviewed by a PSO (Personnel Selection Officer) who would make recommendations as to which Company we should be placed.

And then finally welcome to Egypt.'

Our First Guard Mounting

Only two days in our new abode and some of us are 'selected' for Regimental Guard Mounting.

Corporal Ted Streeter, our old campaigner was to be our Guard Commander and he lost no time in letting us know the various points and intricacies of a Regimental Guard Mount.

Dress was best BD., boots rifle etc. and an absolutely immaculate turnout as we would be inspected by the Duty Officer of the day and the Orderly Sergeant.

Guard Mounting would take place on the Main Square and would follow very traditional regimental drill movements.

We all looked forward to our first Guard with a certain amount of trepidation as we had been told stories of soldiers being marched off the square and 'inside' for a dirty belt or rifle.

In the event it all went off 'peacefully' and we marched off to relieve the old Guard at the Guard Room. Very traditionally we would be on standard 'Stags' that is to say two hours on and four hours off.

My first stag was in a sandbagged trench opposite the main gate. As well as my rifle I had a Bren gun with a fully loaded magazine. All around the perimeter was barbed wire interspersed with rusty old tins, anybody attempting to cross the wire would rattle the cans - well that was the theory.

On my second stag I heard shouting from a trench alongside the main gate. 'Corporal I think someone's trying to come through the wire.' It was certainly rattling.

Ted Streeter came dashing out. 'Don't shoot yet, let me investigate.' With his rifle at the ready he crept up to the wire and shouted out, 'Don't panic, it's only one of those Piard (Desert Dogs) beasts looking for food!'

On our two hours off we were not allowed to undress or even take our boots off. There were metal beds but no mattresses so if you wanted to sleep it was pretty uncomfortable particularly as the lights remained on.

Personnel Selection

The interview was carried out by an officer from HQ Company and was on an individual basis.

Fortunately I had done a little 'Homework' on the structure of the Battalion and had already decided Support Company would be my first choice.

Why was this? Probably because I had discovered that Support Company personnel travelled in carriers and other vehicles as against marching like Rifle Companies!

In the event I get my wish and had a place allocated with the Anti Tank platoon in Support Company.

Support Company lines were directly alongside the Suez perimeter wire, twenty yards from the almost defunct NAAFI, and a couple of hundred yards from the ablutions.

Suez 1952. A typical company lines tented layout.
Note the 'lines' drawn in the sand, a bass broom was used to generate the pattern. Some regiments even used old jerry cans painted white to form a very 'neat' border around their tents!

Each platoon had its own individual tented area, so we had the 3 inch mortar Platoon, MMG (Medium Machine Gun) Platoon, Assault Pioneer Platoon and the 17 Pdr Anti-Tank Platoon.

From memory and identification from photographs the following were also allocated from 51/14 Group to the Anti-Tank Platoon. Ayling, Tony Blunt, John Baigent, Knocker Boiling, Ferdie Croft, Curly Fuller, Arthur Filsell, Bert Gurr, Jim Jeffcoate, John Oliver, Pete Mills, Willie Williams. We were a great group and all mucked in together, and all hailed from Sussex.

Our Platoon Sergeant was 'Wally' Hammond who would be responsible for all our training on the 17 pounder anti tank gun. A very tall and precise NCO he had only recently returned from a 17 pounder anti tank course in the UK. A wonderful instructor with no airs and graces he very soon whipped us into shape.

The 17 pounder we learnt had entered service in 1942 and replaced the 2 and 6 pounder guns in an attempt to combat the ever increasing weight of tank armour.

17 Pounder Anti Tank Gun.

It was extremely accurate and at 800 yards shells would almost enter the same hole, as the previous shell.

Its drawbacks were the weight of 3040kg and the 36" recoil, which caused significant quantities of dust in the desert, which would envelop the gun crew.

To tow our guns we used the WWII American Stuart tanks without the turret. These were powered with two eight cylinder Cadillac engines which gave a tremendous turn of speed even over the roughest desert terrain. Although there were nominated drivers, we all 'had a go' when out on various schemes. It was a delight to drive.

These two photographs show two of the tracked vehicles used to tow the 17pdr. Anti Tank guns.
The top one is a Bren Gun Carrier. It was called 'Tiger-Moth'.
The second is a converted Stuart or Honey Tank. Very fast and powerful it was preferred to the Bren Gun Carrier. Both vehicles are shown loaded onto an LCT and crossing the Suez Ccanal.

Our training, which was over a period of five weeks was extremely well structured. Everything was carried out with drill like precision and we all learnt each role and function of a gun team.

The various roles were layer or aimer, using a telescopic sight to set the range and adjust for any movement of the target.

The loader who pushed home the shell and pulled the lever to fire the shell. The ammunition carrier who carried the required type of shell to the loader. The Detachment Commander, usually a Corporal who would give instructions to the Gun Team.

Such was the training that even today I can recall the sequence of orders to fire the gun.

Detachment Commander: 'Target twelve o'clock moving left'
Layer: 'Traverse left, slow left, on'
Detachment Cmdr: 'Left a half'
Layer: 'Left a half - SET-ON'
Loader: 'In'
Detachment Cmdr: 'Fire'

We also had to learn about the recoil recuperating system which controlled the long recoil of the barrel (piece) and how to remove the breech block and firing mechanism. Also all the various maintenance requirements.

Tank recognition also played a very important part in our training and we had to memorise the silhouettes of all the Russian, American and British tanks.

At the end of our training we towed two of the guns to a special range beneath the Ataqa mountains just west of Suez, where we spent two nights in bivouacs.

The range was littered with redundant WWII Sherman tanks which were to be our targets. In order to make it more realistic we would put a couple of cans of petrol inside the hull of the tank. A direct hit would be registered with an explosion and flash of flame as the jerry cans exploded.

The noise, smoke and recoil when firing an armour piercing shell of 76mm calibre was unbelievable. We had no ear protection whatsoever, and the blast literally pulled back our cheeks and almost pushed your eyes back in their sockets.

The Anti Tank Platoon 'showing off'
in front of a Sherman Tank just decimated!

Although the trail legs of the guns and the spades were imbedded in the sand the gun still jumped around like a dervish, all three tons of it.

In spite of all this it was a wonderful experience and one which I still remember with some pride.

Normal Duties

Back at Camp we became more involved with Support Company. Our Company Commander was Major Morgan and Company Sergeant Major 'Jack' Spratt both Second World War veterans. Major Morgan could often be seen riding his beautifully kept horse around the perimeter wire and would often stop and pass the time of day.

'Jack' Spratt was a huge man in every sense of the word. Apparently he had been a very good boxer and was in fact an ex Imperial Services champion. He also had a delightful way of expressing himself.

For example at Muster Parade one morning he gave us all a dressing down because, as he said, 'Yesterday the Company

Commander and I walked around the Company lines, and I was wiv im - and they was filfy'"

By now we had been issued with the delightful dark green jungle hat and complete sets of Khaki Drill (KD) uniforms.

The jungle hat was so much more versatile than the beret. It could be made into all sorts of different shapes, it kept the sun off and could be easily washed. We all loved it and managed to generate our own particular personality with the shape, some even looking like Al Capone.

This photograph will give an indication of the different 'styling' which could be performed on the very versatile Jungle Hat. Modelling by members of the Anti-tank Platoon!

KD was also something very different. For a start it had to be starched which was a problem in itself as the Dhobi Wallahs (laundry men) had all quit the Camp. There was a small laundry area which still managed to cope with KD for special occasions ie Battalion Headquarters Guard Mounting.

When on Guard Mount you had to be very careful before forming up that you didn't 'crack' the starched creases!

KD consisted of KD shorts, long trousers and KD top. There was also a KD belt for walking out. When wearing shorts we also had to wear hosetops, puttees and boots.

Hosetops were just like long woollen socks but 'cut off' at the ankle. Puttees, which were basically a four inch strip of thick khaki cloth were wound four times around the ankle and the hosetop and fixed with tape fitted to the puttee.

The difficult part to master was ensuring 'wrapping' was incremented in approximately half inch steps up the leg and that the tape finished at an exact position on the outside of the leg.

Fortunately it was only necessary to use hosetops and puttees on certain ceremonial occasions and 'warm weather' Guard Mounting. They were certainly not very practical and appeared to be a leftover from the days of the Raj in India!

We had all been warned about a forthcoming RSM's drill parade which would take place on the Main Square. The purpose of this parade was for the RSM to judge the standard of foot and arms drill of the whole Battalion without the officers.

'Ronnie' Lucas was the Regimental Sergeant Major, small in stature, always immaculately turned out and with a wonderful word of command, he had no problem in drilling a force of over 800 men. He eventually became an officer and ended up with the rank of Major and an MBE.

On the day of the drill parade we all formed up in the company lines and were warned in no uncertain terms what was expected of us - we had been warned!

Once on the square we formed up by Companies and awaited the arrival of the RSM.

His first order was to call us to 'Attention' and then slope arms. The slope was an absolute disaster. There appeared to be a problem with the timing!

Calling a halt to the proceedings he instructed the Company Sergeant Majors to 'sort out the problem' before he continued. It was soon apparent that the problem stemmed from the new recruits 51/14 Group, of which I was of course one. Our drill movements were much slower than the 'old sweats' in the Battalion. Whereas their drill was 1-2-3 ours was still the training rate of 1 - 2 - 3, a significant difference! We soon had it sorted out and found the faster movement much easier than the slower ones.

Ronnie Lucas soon had us moving as one and was satisfied enough to introduce the Band into the programme. The Royal Sussex Band was around fifty strong and really was inspirational to us all when marching around the square in both quick and slow time.

It was here where I heard for the first time the Regimental marches and of course marched for the first time to 'Sussex by the Sea'. It was uplifting to say the least.

I had always assumed that the Regimental march was 'Sussex by the Sea' but this in fact was not. The Regimental march when marching at attention was 'The Royal Sussex' which was combined with the old Second Battalion Regiment march 'Lass of Richmond Hill'. We soon learnt the first colloquial lines which went:-

'The Royal Sussex are leaving today
All the girls in the family way'!

The Regimental slow march was 'Rousillon' a wonderful lilting slow march which again lifted the spirits when marching in Review order.

'Sussex by the Sea' written by W Ward-Higgs in 1907 is the real marching song of the Royal Sussex Regiment.

It was sung with great gusto on Mess nights and more particularly at the end of the annual Royal Sussex Old Comrades reunions.

The following piece taken from a letter in the local Evening Argus in 2001 sums up the emotional aspect of this marching song:-

'One regimental tradition was demonstrated at the end of the meal when, to the music of the Little Common Royal British Legion Band, the assembled veterans rose to their feet and sang Sussex by the Sea.

The passion and raw emotion aroused brought tears to the eye and a lump in the throat.'

R Truelove
(ex-Royal Sussex Regiment)

TROUBLE AT SUEZ

On several nights there had been sporadic shooting heard from the directions of Suez by Egyptian police and civilians. Their targets were the water filtration plant under the guard of our old friends the Buffs and the Suez WD petrol point. All key installations without which it would be very difficult to operate, particularly on the water supply side.

There were concerns that the terrorists had been using a powerful German Spandau machine gun, but this had not been positively identified. The whole Battalion was therefore summoned to attend a special machine gun demonstration in a large pit to the west of the camp.

Two machine guns were used, a Spandau and one of the Battalion's Vickers MMG. The objective was to highlight the difference in the 'sound' of the two machine guns, so that if anybody heard shooting they might be able to confirm the use of a Spandau.

Most of us found the two guns almost identical in sound characteristics, but found the exercise interesting and also showed us a side of the camp we had not previously seen!

December 3rd dawned bright and clear, a normal training day. Around midday the bugle call 'Cromwell' sounded. This was the signal for the 'stand by' company, which on this day was 'B' Company to prepare for action. The whole camp sprang to life as by now the sound of considerable shooting could be heard from the direction of the Suez WD petrol point.

Lts. Blaxter & Gratton celebrating the news that they had received Commendations for their actions during the 'Battle of Suez'.

The shooting became so intense towards the direction of Support Company lines that as we went to the cookhouse for our Tiffin, spent bullets were landing on the sand alongside us. Needless to say we made it to the security of the brick built cookhouse in double quick time. Perhaps we could have claimed to have been under fire!

At four o'clock the carriers from Support Company were called out again as it had been reported that a party of Mauritian soldiers, members of the Pioneer Corps and a Royal Engineers officer had been ambushed at Shell Corner Suez.

When they returned we saw that a total of five dead Mauritians were strapped to the back of the Carriers - not a pretty sight.

The Mortar Platoon on their way to relieve The Buffs who had been 'pinned' down by native fire at the Filtration Plant, Suez.

The guards were doubled that night in the expectation of further trouble but it was a quiet night.

Next day the anti tank platoon was 'selected' to act as a rifle company and was to undergo training to 'relieve' the Buffs from the filtration plant. We were shown a plan of the filtration plant and the positions where terrorists and police had been firing on our troops.

An area was marked in the desert outside the camp the size of the filtration plant and we practised 'storming' it. Fortunately nothing came of it and we were not required and were stood down.

Christmas was a very quiet affair in 1951. With one bottle of beer per man things were not going to get out of hand.

The 3" Mortar Section prepare to bomb Arbein Village where known activists had been shooting our supply columns. They were firing from alongside Support Co. lines, Suez December 1951.

We had a reasonable Christmas dinner which as tradition dictated was served by the officers. Oh, yes and we were served early morning tea 'Gunfire' by our senior NCO's and warrant officers which was quite a treat.

If we thought that we were going to have a quiet new year we were mistaken. On January 3rd and 4th further terrorist attacks took place on No 1 Signal Box, the filtration plant and the WD petrol point.

Much of the shooting had come from the Kafr Abdu village in the Arbein area. Part of the village had been demolished by the Parachute Brigade in December following instructions from General Erskine.

He now ordered the demolition of the remainder of the village. In order to do this the Royal Sussex had to first of all occupy the remainder of the village and build a wire perimeter around it.

At 05.45 hrs on 6th January Support Company including the anti tank platoon moved off to seize and hold the extremities of the village. This we did without any trouble and we remained in our dugouts and sangars for the rest of the day. The only trouble we saw was when a little old lady was allowed in to fetch a few belongings. On her return to the bridge over the Sweetwater Canal she was set upon by the locals, accused of 'fraternising' and her belongings thrown into the Canal.

Kafr Abdu village. General Erskine gave orders for it to be destroyed as it was a Snipers paradise!

To many of us it was our first close up view of the Sweetwater Canal. What a misnomer, it was filthy, basically a cesspit full of rubbish, dead dogs and the like. Amazingly the locals could wash and clean their teeth in the water. We were warned of the dire consequences to our health if we were to fall in!

By 17.10 hrs our work was complete and we withdrew along with the one troop of Centurion tanks from 4 RTR who had joined our force in case of trouble.

It was an interesting exercise which could have gone one way or the other. Certainly with Kafr Abdu village now just rubble the Arbein area was much quieter and the filtration plant no longer under attack.

ISMAILIA - JAN 1952

Towards the middle of January there were rumours of a move from our camp at Suez, nothing was confirmed. However one key indicator according to the 'Old Soldiers' was an increased activity by the Regimental Police in rounding up stray dogs which had been made into pets by many of the soldiers. Sure enough before long the 'Janker Wallahs' were seen digging a large deep pit alongside the old Dakota near the centre of the camp.

Although I didn't witness it myself all stray dogs were apparently put in the pit and shot by sten gun!

On January 19th news filtered through of a shooting incident in Ismailia when two men from the Royal Lincolns were shot dead and six wounded. Also a well respected nun Sister Anthony was shot dead in the same incident when attempting to shepherd some children to safety.

There was a further incident on January 25th when General Erskine gave the order for all Ismailia police to be disarmed.

The Lancashire Fusiliers were given the task of cordoning and disarming but the police refused to budge from their buildings.

Ismailia. The married families NAAFI which was overrun and gutted during the rioting.

There was a good deal of shooting from both sides. Eventually after much skirmishing and some shell fire from the Centurions of 4 RTR the police gave up. Unfortunately there was a grim price to pay for the police lost forty dead and sixty five injured.

Much more trouble was expected from King Farouk in Cairo in light of all this action.

We were as a Regiment put on standby. Our kit bags were packed and stored and were only allowed a small pack with washing gear and a change of clothing plus of course our rifle and bandolier of ammunition.

On January 26th we were told we would be relieved by the Border Regiment who would take over Hodgsons Camp, and we would all be transported to Ismailia.

The Royal Sussex would become a member of 3rd Infantry Brigade together with 1st East Lancs and 1st Lancashire Fusiliers and operate within the Ismailia area.

Ismailia was around fifty miles north of Suez and close to Lake Timsah. When we arrived in our carriers and lorries our Platoon were allocated an area called French Square. It was not to be a permanent site so we had to erect small two man bivouacs in the middle of what was ornamental gardens. All around were very European looking houses which were obviously still occupied by wealthy people.

*Royal Sussex Tactical
H.Q. Provost Sergeant
Paddy Hannafin is in front
holding the Sten Gun.*

*Our tents which were pitched
in the centre of French Square,
Ismailia.*

*Support Company Commander Major Morgan at French Square the
morning after our arrival.*

It was certainly different waking up in the morning in the middle of an ornamental garden, in the centre of town, instead of in the middle of the desert!

Major Morgan and Lt. Gratton being interviewed by the International Press shortly after we had taken over French Square.

Food was brought up in hay boxes and drinking and washing water supplied from a water tanker which used to visit daily.

Muster parades and guard mounting was carried out in a street adjoining French Square. There was no traffic because of the barbed wire cordon and removable barricades.

Eventually the 'outside life' had to come to an end and we were sent to relieve 'C' Company who had been billeted in the Hotel des Voyageurs. The hotel had been requisitioned by the military authorities because of its key position being close to the railway station. Also the Avenue on which the hotel was sited separated Arab town from the European quarter.

Our main task was the protection of the European population and the cordoning of the Arab quarter at night.

It was whilst in the hotel that I had a really frightening experience. I had come off guard and decided to clean my rifle which had been checked to be empty and deposited in the Guard Room.

I withdrew my rifle, signing for it and went up to our 'barrack rooms' which had around twelve others from my platoon. For some reason I worked the bolt and squeezed the trigger. There was a resounding explosion and a bullet from my rifle hit the cornicing on the ceiling. Of course all hell let loose, everybody came rushing in, the Guard Commander inspected my rifle and found four other live rounds in the magazine. Fortunately all records indicated that my rifle had been 'cleared' when I had checked it into the Guard rooms.

So what could have happened? Maybe someone had withdrawn the wrong rifle, loaded the magazine with five rounds as standard practice, realised their mistake and put it back into the rifle rack.

Fortunately for me the incident was not pursued and not reported.

The Avenue, Ismailia, as viewed from the railway station. This avenue separated Arab Town and the European Quarter, which was why it was so strategically important. Our Platoon were billeted in 'The Hotel des Voyageurs', which can be seen halfway down on the left of the Avenue.

Probably because we were on detachment helped, and because we were a self-contained unit, just a platoon at that time, and nobody was hurt, although they could have been.

I felt particularly sorry for Tom P who was on the next bed to me. He had just spent some time 'inside' for accidentally shooting a colleague in the foot whilst on sentry duty. He went absolutely white!

Downstairs in the hotel lounge there was a 'wind up' gramophone with one record, which was played incessantly. I remember particularly one side which was 'Life's a Golden Dream'. For me to hear that tune brings back instant memories of Ismailia and more particularly the Hotel des Voyageurs.

On the roof of the Hotel des Voyageurs.
Back row = Boiling, Fuller, Croft, Masters, Troak, Williams
Front row = Blunt, Gurr, Vaughan, Ayling.

The tension at the end of January had eased considerably, mainly because King Farouk had got personally involved and sacked his minister Nahas for 'his failure to keep order'.

Our Anti tank platoon therefore moved down the road to take up residence in some splendid wooden chalets which formed part of Timsah leave camp. Surrounded by beautiful trees and almost on Lake Timsah it was an idyllic site.

It was whilst we were at Timsah that we heard of the death of King George VI, the first news we had received from the UK for three months!

All our anti tank guns had been sited overlooking the Suez Canal at a place called Ferry Point. We used to get trucked down there daily to clean the guns and carry out certain drills. It was very pleasant watching the ships pass through the Canal as, stripped to the waist, we carried out our duties.

FERRY POINT AND NORTH CAMP

But guess what? After a few days at Timsah leave camp we were on the move again. Tented accommodation had been found for us at Ferry Point quite close to our guns and to Battalion HQ.

It was at Ferry Point where the Battalion held a very moving memorial service for the late His Majesty King George VI. Very fittingly, during the service a ship passed silently through the Canal on its way to Port Said.

The news of the death of His Majesty the King was received with profound sorrow. It was, however, heartening to see the Egyptian flags lowered to half-mast despite the strained relations prevailing at the time.

Memorial service for His late Majesty King George VI
at Ferry Point, February 1952.
The picture is of the parade service with members of H.Q. and
support companies.

On another occasion when we were working in the gun park we suddenly heard a band playing 'Sussex by the Sea'. It appeared to be coming from the Canal and it was. Passing through the Canal was the light fleet aircraft carrier HMS Ocean. On the flight deck was the on board Royal Marine Band who had kindly struck up 'Sussex by the Sea'. Boy, didn't we feel good, but also a little homesick for our home county.

An item of relief during the period was the passage through the Canal of H.M.S. Ocean – a light fleet aircraft carrier. As it passed Ferry Point the Royal Marine Band most kindly struck up 'Sussex by the Sea' on the flight deck, a gesture much appreciated by all ranks and for which a signal expressing our thanks was made to the Captain by the Commanding Officer.

By the end of April 1952 we had got pleasantly used to Ferry Point and its close proximity to the ever changing Canal. The trees were really magnificent and great for shelter from the midday sun, water was plentiful and duties not too onerous.

The Suez Canal from our camp at Ferry Point.

So what did we do? We moved again, this time to take over North Camp from the 1st Royal Lincolns. The obvious advantage from a Battalion perspective was that the whole regiment would once more be together as a unit, instead of being located by company all around Ismailia.

North Camp

The disadvantage was the camp. There appeared to be no solid buildings, only tented accommodation. Water was virtually non-existent and toilet facilities were to say the least primitive. In fact one of the first jobs was to construct more suitable toilets for each of the company lines.

Suez 1952. Digging the 'pit', this being the first and most important stage in the construction of a typical Suez toilet block.

As I remember it ours was a rectangular pit dug in the sand approximately 15ft (450cm) x 8ft deep (240cm). On top of this the regiment pioneers constructed a long wooden box, obviously well supported with 10" round holes (25cm) cut in the top. From memory there were six 'holes' in our block.

The whole construction was covered with Hessian sacking supported by timber supports. For modesty a Hessian screen separated each of the holes and they were definitely an improvement to those we had taken over!

Whilst at North Camp I had my first experience of a British Military Hospital (BMH). I had developed a very bad case of Foot Rot (Athlete's Foot) in my left foot. The orderlies in our medical inspection room had tried to clean it up with Permanganate of Potash solution - the normal treatment - but it appeared to be resistant to their efforts.

Accordingly, the Medical Officer arranged for me to go to BMH Fayid, the military hospital for the Canal Zone. The consultant doctor at the hospital was confident he could clear it up, but recommended I should spend four days with nothing on my feet, not even bed covers.

Within two days my foot had virtually cleared up and looked really good. However I had noticed a yellow encrustation had developed in my scalp which I immediately reported to the senior male nurse. He diagnosed impetigo, probably 'picked up' from a dirty pillow in the ward! The treatment - to have my hair shaved so that a special ointment could be applied. Out came the scissors and electric razor and in no time my head was as shiny as the day I was born!

In twenty-four hours the impetigo had disappeared and I was left with a bald head.

The sequel to this was that when I got back to camp and went into the cookhouse for a meal I decided to wear my hat. I was very conscious of my bald and shiny head. Hats are not allowed in the cookhouse, which I knew but decided to take a chance and wear mine.

Unfortunately, the orderly sergeant was carrying out his duties and asking 'any complaints?' when he spotted me with my hat on.

'Get that hat off!' he bellowed.

I replied, 'It's medical, sergeant.'

'Take it off' he insisted.

I did and exposed my shiny head.

'Yes I see what you mean, you had better keep it on, it certainly improves your appearance.' He said.

Just imagine going into hospital with bad feet and coming out bald!

Today nobody would 'turn a hair' to see a shaven head, but in the early 1950s the term 'Skinhead' had not been invented.

Fayid 1952.
K.D. Walking Out Dress.

Whilst at North Camp, Battalion training was stepped up. It had been almost four months since the regiment was under 'one roof' and virtually no detailed training had been carried out. To conclude the training the Battalion went on a five day scheme into the desert.

For many of us it was the first opportunity to 'discover' the desert and to sleep under the stars. From our platoon's point of view it was a wonderful opportunity to tow our 17 pounder guns in real sandy conditions.

We soon learnt the meaning of 'dig in and brew up.' To boil our water for tea etc. we were taught how to make a Bengazi stove, developed by the Desert Rats during the Second World War. It was simple really, take an old large Bully Beef can or similar. Half fill with sand. Take a jerry can of 80 octane fuel and pour on the sand. Put a match to it and bingo, you have a wonderful stove.

Stop and brew up!
17Pdr and Stuart Carrier. Crew comprises:
Boiling, Fuller, Lucas, Ayling, Cpl. Samuels, Jenkins.

The scheme was operational night and day for the whole of the five days. How it was all organised I just do not know. Sometimes we would be woken up at say two o'clock in the morning, pack up our gear, hitch the guns to the carriers and head off to some distant wadi, dig in, camouflage up and wait for the next instruction. Obviously somebody knew what was going on and where some eight hundred men were located, and what our next movement were to be. I can remember we went to a place called Kidney Ridge and to another Gebel Iweibid. deep in the desert. We had maps of a sort but navigation was quite difficult because of the lack of any real features on the featureless landscape.

Laying on to a target in the Sinai Desert.

Anyway we all got back in one piece and as a platoon we got to know each other a great deal better.

SHANDUR

Back at North Camp we had gradually improved conditions somewhat. So what happened? After two months we moved on again. This time to Cambrai Camp, Shandur where the regiment took over from the 3rd Parachute Regiment. The camp was promptly renamed Gibraltar Lines.

Certainly it was a much better camp with permanent buildings for the offices and stores. We were still under canvas but in a more suitable location. There was even a YMCA adjacent to the camp where we could get a decent meal and watch a film albeit in the open air.

It was around this time that many of the regulars indicated that they should hear about going back to the UK because their PYTHON was up. What they were saying was that their three years overseas tour was nearing completion.

Unfortunately, and I had a lot of sympathy for them, their tour of duty was extended for a further six months because of the Suez situation.

This did give us all an indication that there was a possibility that the whole Battalion could go back to the UK in early 1953. That would certainly suit me.

By this time most of us were now speaking the language of the Battalion, which was a smattering of Arabic and Indian. This had been evolved over many years following the regiment's tours of duty in India and most of the Middle Eastern countries. For example:

Malish	-	It doesn't matter
Quois Quiteer	-	Very good
Yalla	-	Push off
Tiffin	-	Cold lunch
Charpoy	-	Bed
Bondook	-	Rifle
Charwallah	-	Tea boy
Ala Keefik	-	I don't care

And of course there were many slang words and words that were a derivition of Hindustani and Arabic.

It was all very easy to pick up and was probably helped by the fact that we were all in close proximity to each other in an enclosed camp.

Another thing which manifested itself once we were back in a more permanent camp was the 'Demob Chart'. Some of the National Servicemen in my group I knew had commenced a Demob Chart from Day one. Simply, this consisted of a two year calendar on which each passing day towards demob was struck off. To me not an exercise worth pursuing but others thought differently.

As the time for demob got ever closer the 'Demob Happy' soldier would shout to his mate 'How long now?' Back would come the reply, for example 'Eight weeks, three days, ten hours and an early breakfast.' On demob day, which was inevitably at the depot in the UK, a soldier would be allowed to have an early breakfast so that he could catch the early train home.

All around the training depot one would hear shouts such as 'one day and an early breakfast' - we still had twenty-three months to do!

Our 51/14 group had celebrated its first anniversary - the first twelve months service completed when some of us were 'approached' to see whether we would be interested in signing on as regular soldiers.

I personally was spoken to by our platoon Sergeant, 'Struttie' Struthers, who told me I would be a full corporal in three months and a Sergeant in twelve months if I signed. I declined and as far as I knew not one of our group became a regular soldier.

However, there was still a lot of pressure to come. I was offered a Brigade level course on the 17 Pounder Anti tank gun which was only normally offered to NCOs.

*All camouflaged
and waiting to fire!*

I, of course, accepted as I was interested in learning more about the 17 pounder and it would give me a whole week away from the Regiment. The course was to be held at the Camp of the 1st East Lancs and would be conducted by an army staff instructor from Warminster, UK.

I was to attend with Corporal 'Geordie' Allsopp, a regular soldier from our platoon. When we arrived for the pre-instruction briefing there were four full corporals from the East Lancs and four from the Lancashire Fusiliers. I was the only private. This could have been embarrassing particularly as we had been invited to use the facilities of the East Lancs corporal's mess. The answer was simple for the duration of the course, I would be loaned a couple of stripes - Corporal Troak (temporary) what easy promotion, although illegal!

It was a most interesting course which ended with both a written and oral test for all concerned. I came second in the results which I was pleased with and before we departed for our various camps I was told by the Staff Instructor that he would personally recommend me for promotion to at least a Lance Corporal.

As promised he must have sent in his report and recommendations because within a couple of weeks I was summoned to meet the Adjutant. Did I have a Field Marshall's Baton in my small pack, I asked myself.

The Adjutant's Office was based in HQ Lines an area where I had never ventured before, and I went with some trepidation - adjutants are usually considered pretty fearsome characters.

In the event I had nothing to fear, the Adjutant was perfectly charming. He said he had received a glowing report on my recent Brigade Course and mentioned the recommendation for promotion to an NCO. Would I be interested and if I was he would put forward his recommendation. He also pointed out that I would have to attend the next RSM's NCOs Drill Cadre which was always very testing.

I agreed I would like to proceed, which he said he would action, then he asked me whether or not I had considered signing on as a regular soldier!

Within two days there was a notice on Part 1, orders that Private M Troak was promoted to Acting unpaid Lance Corporal, it was certainly unpaid!

The RSM's Drill Cadre

The RSM Mr Lucas in earshot, Ronnie out of earshot, was a real disciplinarian in terms of drill, and a master of the pace stick.

I once had the 'privilege' of watching him drill some of the junior officers on the finer points of Sword Drill. We were not supposed to have been watching but we happened to be in the vicinity

Some of the junior subalterns were obviously in fear of Ronnie Lucas's cutting remarks but he had no fears of the officer's rank.

I remember him saying to one Second Lieutenant 'Mr C your sword is wobbling like a jelly, I would kindly suggest that you hold it steady, sir,' with heavy emphasis on the 'Sir'.

The RSM's junior NCOs cadre which I was to attend was for five days. I was warned by one of the corporals who had previously attended to ensure that all of my kit was absolutely immaculate and that I turned up early.

Sure enough on the first morning we were thoroughly inspected by the RSM and many things were found wanting.

The course was mainly to teach us how to drill other soldiers and this was the main thrust.

Under Ronnie's watchful eye we had to individually drill the remainder of the cadre. This of course necessitated a good loud word of command, how did we achieve this? Simple really - we were split into two sections and lined up around twenty yards apart and had to shout orders at one another. This would usually last half an hour or until our throats were shot! We were also taken through the history of the regiment and in particular the list of the VCs awarded to members of the regiment.

One particular point of interest was being taken to the mess and viewing the wonderful display of regimental silver. It was truly magnificent and of course beautifully kept.

There was no written exam at the end of the course, only the RSMs written assessment of each individual. I am glad to say I passed.

Summer At Shandur

For many of us National Servicemen this was to be our first summer in Egypt and didn't it get hot.

Because of the afternoon heat we would have a much earlier Reveille, then work through the morning until lunchtime.

A creature of the Sinai Desert.

After lunch we were basically finished unless we were on specific duties. It was so hot under the canvas of our tents that we would simply lay out on our beds with just shorts on and the mosquito net over us. It wasn't so much the 'mossies' but more the flies, they were terrible.

Fayid 1952. Camel, Troak and 'Curly' Fuller.

Drinking water was stored in tall clay pots, chatti's, I believe they were called. Placed in the shade they somehow kept the water remarkably cool.

With all the flies, sand and poor sanitary conditions we were constantly warned about the need for good hygiene. Unfortunately it didn't always work; the camp was struck down with a severe bout of Paratyphoid 'B'. It had apparently started in the cookhouse, probably from the wrong preparation of the lettuce and unclean hands.

The entire cookhouse staff were removed and replaced with a new batch from another regiment. At the same time our NAAFI was also closed. I understand that at least fifty percent of the regiment was struck down, some so bad that they had to go into hospital.

The cure if not badly affected was a hundred or so of large white pills which had to be swallowed with copious amounts of water.

Fortunately, I managed to escape the dreaded para, which wasn't much help really because with so many struck down with it, the duties and guards had to be shared among less people. No escape for the healthy!

Ted Vaughan

Whilst at Shandur our platoon suffered a terrible, tragic loss. Ted Vaughan, a very popular 'regular' from our platoon was electrocuted whilst operating a potato peeling machine in the cookhouse. Apparently the switch to operate the machine was faulty. Ted had 'ammo' boots on and was standing in water. In those conditions death was instant.

I had got to know Ted very well as he had been my carrier driver on many of the schemes in the desert. He hailed from Uckfield, was a very keen racing cyclist and had won many races in the locality.

On schemes he was an absolute boon, he was a very good cook and could produce almost gourmet meals from our limited 'compo' ration.

Ted died on 29th November 1952 and was buried at Fayid War Cemetery with full military honours. It was a very moving service and burial and one I have never forgotten.

Major Sleeman, Lt. Stephenson, John Baigent.

The funeral of Cpl. Ted Vaughan.

Ted was buried with full Military Honours at Fayid Military Cemetery.

He died as a result of an electrical accident in the cookhouse at Shandur Camp.

In 1997 Jess Taylor who was part of 51/14 group, visited the Canal Zone with a group of Suez veterans. He visited and paid his respects at Ted Vaughan's grave in Fayid. Naturally he took photographs of the headstone and when he returned home he wrote to the local press offering copy photos for any of Ted's relatives.

There was almost an instant response from a brother and other relatives. It became apparent to Jess during his conversation with the family that they knew little or nothing about the circumstances leading to Ted's death. So, at least Jess was able to 'tie up' some of the loose ends, and give some comfort to the family that Ted had been given a fitting military funeral.

The Desert Rose

In various parts of the camp there were single urinals. These were basically a metal tube going into the sand with a funnel at the top approximately 2ft 6 inches (75 cms) above ground level. A hessian modesty screen was fitted around the 'Rose'. These urinals would be used by both officers and other ranks.

The other ranks felt a real sense of achievement if when passing one of these Desert Roses they found one being used by an officer, because they would salute him. Of course, the officer would have to respond with his one free hand! I think they, or at least some of them, saw the funny side!

4

HOMEWARD BOUND?

Just before Christmas 1952 rumours started to circulate around the camp that the Royal Sussex would definitely be returning to the UK in the early part of 1953. Of course, we had heard these sorts of rumours before. 'Duff gen' was a way of life and taken with a 'pinch of salt' could often enliven a boring day.

However, on this occasion it was confirmed that an advance party would definitely be leaving to set up our next Barracks in the UK. So things did seem to be on the move.

Sure enough shortly after Christmas we were all informed that we would be on our way at the end of January, further details to follow.

Yes, Homeward Bound

January 28th, 1953 was the date given to us to sail back to the UK. The troopship allocated to the Battalion was the Empire Ken. Those of us who had travelled from Trieste on the deplorable Empire Test hoped it would not be a 'sister ship' in every sense of the word.

A great spirit pervaded the camp during January particularly from the regulars who would be going home for the first time in three years.

From a support company point of view there was not a great deal of pre-packing required as our anti tank guns and equipment would be left behind in Shandur, it was only our personal kit which we had to take care of.

At last the great day arrived and we left Shandur at 07:15 arriving at Adabiya docks, Suez at 09:00. We had to be ferried out to the Empire Ken on large landing craft which was quite an experience itself.

*The Troopship Empire Ken which was our 'home' for
eleven days on our journey back to the U.K.*

The Empire Ken, we established was a much younger ship than the
Empire Test. It had been built in Germany in 1928, slightly larger
than the Test. She was powered by four steam turbines. Although
sleeping accommodation was in hammocks there was still a fair
amount of room either side of one's 'bed space'.

During the voyage we all had to wear plimsolls. The reason
for this as explained to me by a member of the crew was:

1. They didn't want their decks scuffed with ammo boot
   studs!
2. You would probably be able to swim better with plimsolls
   than boots in the unlikely event of falling overboard.

The regiment gradually arrived company by company until
everybody was on board. At 17:00 hours, just as it was getting dark,
the Captain gave the order to cast off and we were on our way for
the one hundred mile journey up the Suez Canal, to Port Said, and
then onwards to Southampton and home.

I think without exception, as we cast off, everybody was
lining the rails and waving farewell to Egypt. We were rather
disappointed that we were to pass through the Canal at night and
visibility would be restricted. So much of our time over the last

fourteen months had been spent on the banks of the Canal that we would have loved to have waved to the squaddies still there, and given them a soldier's farewell!

Were we sorry to leave? I suppose the real answer is no, you can't beat your home country. We had put up with a lot of hardships and constant moving from camp to camp. However, I believe this had built up a tremendous camaraderie between us all.

It must also not be forgotten that in the period of the 'Suez troubles' from October 1951 to March 1952 fifty four British servicemen were killed and sixty nine seriously injured. So obviously wives, girlfriends and families would be delighted to know we were on our way home, and safe.

As one of the advance party in the UK wrote in the Roussillon Gazette:

> 'Here's to the how and the why and the when, and all God-speed to the Empire Ken.'

We were scheduled to arrive on Saturday 7th February which meant we would be spending eleven days on board (Current flying time six hours!)

The food served on board was really first class, particularly when compared to what we had become used to in Egypt. There was fresh white bread baked on board every day with real butter. Fried eggs were properly cooked without any of the 'black bits' and congealed yolks, and we could have as many as we liked. In fact with the amount of food on offer it really appeared that we were being 'fattened up' before setting foot in the UK!

There was even a cinema on board and I can remember watching the 'Outlaw and the Lady' as one of the films.

Duties were few and far between and apart from the odd fire piquet we were left very much to our own devices. In fact it was a pretty uneventful trip, even the notorious Bay of Biscay was kind to us and remained very flat. The only thing we began to feel was the cold.

ARRIVAL IN SOUTHAMPTON

It was a very cold but sunny afternoon on 7th February 1953 when our troopship, the Empire Ken finally docked at Southampton. We were all on deck and all wearing our wonderful Army great coats to combat the cold as the ship docked to a tumultuous reception. The band was of course playing Sussex by the Sea, the regimental flag was proudly flying at the masthead and the assembled families and friends were soon cheering madly.

There was a whole crowd of dignitaries including the Colonel of the Regiment and mayors from several Sussex towns, all who came on board.

Welcome Home!
Friends and relatives welcome HMT. Empire Ken as she docks at
a cold Southampton on 7 February 1953.

Unfortunately, we had to sleep a further night on board before leaving by special train to Ludgershall, Wilts.

Sunday 8th was again particularly cold, especially so to us old 'desert rats'. We had to clear customs which was not a problem we had been told to expect and board the train which was waiting at the quayside.

Our final destination was to the Fowler Barracks, Perham Down where the advance party would be waiting to welcome us.

Upon arriving at the very small station of Ludgershall we were met by the band of the 2nd Battalion, The Royal Welch Fusiliers, who would be leading us on our march into our new barracks.

There was quite a contingent waiting on the main square at Fowler Barracks to direct and escort us to our various billets. These were mainly new intakes of National Servicemen who had completed their training just before we had left Egypt.

Everything was exceedingly well organised, so much so that we were all paid and cleared to go on four weeks leave on the same day, wonderful!

I think this poem, taken from an issue of the Roussillion Gazette, sums up our feelings as National Servicemen on returning from Egypt.

Return Of The Fighting Men

Who are these fine stalwart heroes standing,
Sun-bronzed and fit, with bold flashing eye,
Scorning the stay-at-home, decrepit Depot
Permanent Staff who chance to pass by.

What is this language these heroes are speaking?
A strange-sounding tongue to our dull Sussex ear.
Words of a wild and magnificent grandeur:
'Malish' and 'Akkers; Imshi; Quois quiteer.'

Whence comes this sand that flies over the Depot
As kit bags are opened and parcels untied;
Whence come these shoes of outrageous pattern,
With soles of thick crepe about four inches wide.

And what of these wild tales of murder and pillage
Stories of bloodshed that grip and enthral,
Recalled from the mem'ry of unceasing service -
Eighteen whole months on the Suez Canal.

Then listen ye weak ones, ye home service details,
Ye broken-down oldsters left high on the shelf,
I'll tell ye the secret - the breath-taking secret -
A draft of NS men have come home from MELF.
JG

Malish =	It doesn't matter
Akkers =	Money
Imshi =	Go away
Quois quiteer =	Very nice

SOLDIERING IN THE UK

Our four weeks leave passed very quickly and all too soon we were reporting back to our new camp at Fowler Barracks, Perham Down, Wilts.

However, from my own personal point of view my horizon was limited by the fact that there was only just under four months and an 'early breakfast' of my two year's service remaining.

Fowler Barracks was very basic, it had been some sort of Hospital during the Second World War. Everything was 'spread out', Support Company was based in wooden huts at the far end of the barracks, adjacent to the carrier park.

There were plenty of new young 'faces' when we arrived back, mainly National Service drafts who had been 'held back' awaiting the Battalion's arrival from Egypt, and we of course wasted no time in recounting our experiences in the desert!

The Queen's coronation on June 2nd was high on the agenda as the Battalion was to supply three hundred men to either line the route or act as a police reserve contingent. The colour party would also be marching the route with both the Regimental and Queen's colours, plus an armed escort.

Most of Support Company was 'selected' for the Coronation detail. As we would be wearing No 1 Dress we all had to be measured for our new uniform which apparently were to be all individually tailored.

There was also at the same time a change to the shoulder tabs on our battle dresses. The Royal Sussex were allowed to change from those used by the Infantry, which were white lettering on a red background to the Regimental colours of royal blue and orange. At the same time we were all issued for the first time with royal blue and orange lanyard, which really did look smart.

In April rumours started to circulate about another move - not again! Sure enough, on May 9th we took over the Assaye Barracks from the 2nd Royal Welch Fusiliers in Tidworth just a few miles down the road from Fowler Barracks.

Our regimental band played us in as we marched through the main gate to our 'new' home.

The Assaye Barracks were one of the army's more modern blocks with really excellent facilities and quite close to a few shops and pubs.

Hopefully, with only nine weeks and an early breakfast this should be 51/14 draft's last move, our tenth in twenty two months.

One of the great advantages of being based in Tidworth was that we could get back to Sussex relatively easily even for a short weekend.

Local coaches would collect us from the barracks at around midday on a Saturday and drive us down to the Palace Pier at Brighton. The average driving time was around three hours.

The coaches were not particularly comfortable being basically old fashioned charabancs, no heating or other comforts, but they were cheap!

On Sunday night the coach would be waiting for us at 11:30pm, again outside the Palace Pier and take us back to Tidworth arriving around three o'clock in the morning. With Reveille at 6.00am it was a very short night!

It was whilst at Tidworth that Support Company was 'selected' to become infantryment for a three day scheme on the notorious Salisbury Plain.

There was a 'plot' for the whole proceedings which basically meant we had to dig defensive slit trenches and prepare for an attack by the 51st Highland Division TA.

We had already received terrible tales of this TA division, of how they had captured a certain RSM and tied him up to a tree for twelve hours. By all accounts they were a pretty unruly mob!

We dug out slit trenches which in the event were like large gun pits. The officer commanding our area was not amused even when our CO explained we were only temporary infantrymen, and that we had been used to digging large gun pits, and not trenches.

Then the rains came. Hours and hours of it, sweeping in across the plain. Before long our trenches were full of water as were we. At night fall we were fortunately 'stood down' as the action had moved elsewhere, and we could step out of our trenches leaving the water behind.

Our Company Sergeant Major, one of the old school, who we inevitably called 'Sponge Nose' because of his very pitted nose, told us to light as large a fire as we could in order to dry out. Then miracle of miracles he arrived with a porcelain jar which was full of rum, just what we wanted.

Each of us was given an issue which was poured into our aluminium mess tins, and never was a drink so welcome and so warming.

When we arrived back at Tidworth we were told that over the next two days we would be required to have the first fitting of our No 1 uniforms for the Coronation. None of us should leave camp as we could be required at very short notice. This basically gave us licence to do nothing for two days, which was brilliant after the Salisbury Plains experience.

I was called in for my 'fitting' on the second day, and to my delight everything fitted perfectly. The uniform was navy blue (Blues) with a red stripe down the outside of each trouser leg. This was reflected in the peak cap which had a red band around it. For walking out there was a blue belt with polished buckle and for the Coronation a white blancoed belt with a heavy embossed brass buckle.

*Assaye Barracks,
Tidworth, May 1953.*

*I am wearing the No.1
dress uniform which had
been specifically made
for the Coronation. On
parade we had white
blancoed belts, rifle
slings and bayonet frogs.*

I also learnt that after the Coronation I was one of the 156 selected to carry out other ceremonial duties in Sussex. These would be in Brighton, Lewes and Eastbourne and we would be based in Warren Camp, Crowborough, for six days.

CORONATION DUTIES

Our base was to be in Kensington Gardens and under canvas for the duration of our time in London.

Lieutenant Colonel JB Ashworth DSO was in charge of our contingent and he regularly came round to see how we were getting along.

Kensington Gardens, our base for the Coronation, June 1953.

The food arranged by the Army Catering Corps was absolutely first class as were the facilities for washing etc. It was a little difficult to manage to maintain good creases in our No 1 uniform under a tent but we did.

June 2nd, Coronation Day, dawned bright and early for all those involved in the public duties.

After a very early reveille and splendid breakfast we formed up in Kensington Gardens resplendent in our No 1 Blues and white blancoed belts.

I remember the streets were very busy with spectators forming up early, and also still plenty of people in sleeping bags on the streets.

One very humorous incident occurred as we were marching at our regulation pace down to the centre of London. The loudspeakers which were strung across the road suddenly struck up with 'Oranges and Lemons'. Of course, this completely put us out of step because it was being played at twice the speed of our marching. For a few minutes until one of the Sergeants called out the pace we looked like a bunch of raw recruits.

As we took up our positions behind the first line of those already lining the route the skies started to change and large black clouds appeared.

As we stood in line there was a sound of cheering coming from our right, the direction from which the Coronation party would come. As we looked we could see a Corporation street cleaner with his metal barrow sweeping up and really playing up to the crowd. He loved it and we loved it.

Then the rains came and didn't it rain. Obviously there was no shelter whatsoever, our brand new uniforms became soaked and we had white blanco running off our webbing. Fortunately we were allowed in rotation to go to the little cafes at the back of our position and buy a very warming cup of tea.

From where I was positioned I was able to see everything and everybody involved in the main procession, even the Royal Sussex Colour party which consisted of ten members of the regiment. The Queen's colour was carried by Lieut. Mike Brady and the Regimental Colour by our own Platoon Commander, Lieut John Stephenson.

The Royal Sussex Colour Party, the Coronation, 2 June 1953.

Major R B de F Sleeman OBE. MC., Lt. M Brady, Lt. J Stephenson, RSM. R Lucas, C/Sgt. O'Brien, Sgt. Barnes, Sgt. Lewis, Cpl. Ashenden, L/Cpl. Catt, Pte. Collinson

It was a really spectacular day and one I personally would not have missed for the world and, of course, it didn't end there, most of us spent the rest of the day and night down in the West End where we were really well treated by all and sundry.

Next day it was back to basics. Still in tents in Kensington Gardens, the one hundred and fifty six of us who had been 'selected' for the Sussex tour had some training to do.

As there would be a considerable amount of marching involved we had to learn the drill of 'Changing arms on the march'.

Once we had drawn our rifles from the security store training started in earnest, much to the amusement of the walkers and bystanders in the park.

Up and down the park, past the Statue of Peter Pan, over the Serpentine, we changed arms, left to right, right to left whilst still marching, until we had it perfect. I must say that once we were in Sussex we were glad we had learnt and practised this particular drill movement, as we used it many times marching through the three towns.

THE SUSSEX TOUR AND FAREWELL TO ARMS

The wet weather experienced during the Coronation had now completely disappeared and we were glad to leave London for sunny Sussex. As a detachment we left on Friday 5th June to take up residence in Warren Camp on the western outskirts of Crowborough.

It was a rambling First World War style of army camp but we were made very comfortable and certainly well fed.

Our first official duty as a Regiment was to receive the Freedom of Lewes on the afternoon of Saturday 6th June. There were huge crowds lining the streets as we marched through the town with bands playing, colours flying and bayonets fixed. There was obviously still a great deal of euphoria following the Coronation celebrations, and this was reflected in the crowd's enthusiasm.

Freedom of Lewes.
The High Sheriff of Sussex, Captain Wethey, R.N., inspects the
parade during the presentation of the Honorary Freedom of the
Borough of Lewes to the Regiment on 6 June 1953.

After all the pomp and circumstance we were all treated to a really delightful 'high tea' in the Lewes Town Hall.

Our next engagement was in Eastbourne on Sunday 7th June when we participated in a large Coronation Thanksgiving service which was held at the Saffrons.

After the service we marched through the town again with bayonets fixed, colours flying and bands playing in front of very large crowds of both locals and holidaymakers.

Once again we were treated to a wonderful tea by the Mayor of Eastbourne in the Town Hall.

Our third and final ceremonial parade was in Brighton on Tuesday 9th June.

As the Regiment had already received the Freedom of Brighton some years before there were certain formalities to perform on the boundary of Brighton and Hove. This was reported in the Brighton and Hove Herald in the following manner:

March through Brighton.
The band and drums at the Borough Boundary
during the march of the detachment of the 1st Battalion
through Brighton on 9 June, 1953.

The thousands of people who stopped and gazed as a
company of soldiers, smart in their full-dress uniforms,
marched along Brighton sea front on Tuesday afternoon
headed by their band, were not watching just a company of
soldiers and their band.
They were a detachment of the 1st Battalion of the Royal
Sussex Regiment, who have the Freedom of the Borough,
and as their commanding officer Lt. Col JB Ashworth said
to the Mayor (Ald J E Hay), who challenged them at the
Hove boundary:

'Have I your permission to enter Brighton with band
playing, colours flying and bayonets fixed, as is the
regiment's right as a Freeman of the Borough?'

Once again we were invited to take tea with the Mayor of Brighton which was served in the dining room of the Black Rock Swimming Pool, now sadly demolished.

On Wednesday 10th June we journeyed back to our barracks in Tidworth having spent over a week on ceremonial duties. Those of us in 51/14 group were determined to keep a 'low profile' as we only had thirty five days and an early breakfast before we would be demobbed and back in Civvy Street.

Our anti tank platoon commander, Lieutenant John Stephenson, wrote in the Rousillon Gazette shortly before our departure:

> 'Within the next few weeks National Service Group 51/14, the last of our desert warriors will go on release. This will leave the platoon commander ample scope to 'shoot lines' about the Mystic East to the new members of the platoon.'

Eventually Thursday 16th July arrived and our 'Early Breakfast'. Although our two years with the Colours was completed there still remained three years and six months Territorial service to complete.

On 'demob' day we had to take all of our kit with us as this would be required for our Territorial duties and would be kept at home. We then had to report to whichever Territorial Headquarters we had been assigned.

In my case with many of my colleagues we had to report to 4/5th Royal Sussex TA Headquarters Bulverhythe near Hastings. From my point of view this was a bit of a pain because it meant travelling from one end of Sussex to the other and then returning back to Brighton.

However we were about to be demobbed so it didn't really matter. After completing lots of forms at Bulverhythe I was told to report to 4/5 Royal Sussex TA Preston Barracks, Brighton, where guess what, they had an anti tank platoon! However that is all another story.

Army Book 111

№ 368590

Surname and Initials _TROAIK. M._

Army No. _22501170_

Group No. _5/14_

DISCHARGE

of a National Service Soldier from
Whole-Time Military Service

> Any person finding this book is requested
> to hand it in to any Barracks, Post Office
> or Police Station, for transmission to the
> Under-Secretary of State, The War Office,
> London, S.W. 1

*Farewell
to Arms
16 July 1953*

Designation of HQ, SR or TA Unit to which the soldier
will report

4/5 (CP) Bn. ROYAL SUSSEX REGT

TA CENTRE

BULVERHYTHE

Date due to report _ST. LEONARDS on-SEA_
_16-7-53_   _SUSSEX._

I have often been asked, did I enjoy my two years of National Service. The answer is always yes. I still meet some of my old 'Muckers' and reminisce about our time together. The 'bad times' in hindsight were not too bad, and the good times wonderful. I was extremely fortunate in seeing quite a large piece of the world and also always on the move and not just based in one location.

At this time, fifty years on, moves are still being made in an attempt to have an award of a general service medal to those who served in the Armed Forces in the Suez Canal zone from 1951 to 1954.

From my point of view this would be the icing on the cake - we will just wait and see!

'And when you go to Sussex
Whoever you may be.
You can tell them all that we stand or fall
For Sussex by the Sea'

APPENDIX I

MILITARY RECORD OF THE AUTHOR
22508130 Sergeant Malcolm Allan Troak

Deemed to have been enlisted for Whole-time Service under the
National Service Acts into the Royal Sussex Regiment
and posted to Depot   26.07.51
Posted to 1st Battalion   26.11.51
Discharged on termination of Whole-time National
Service   09.08.53
Deemed to have been enlisted for Part-time National
Service into the Royal Sussex Regiment Territorial
Army and posted to 4/5th Battalion   10.08.53
Promoted Corporal   19.06.54
Transferred to the Royal Engineers Army Emergency
Reserve and posted to 136 Construction Regiment   29.08.54
Discharged on re-enlistment   20.06.56
Re-enlisted into the Royal Engineers Army
Emergency Reserve and posted to 136 Construction
Regiment   21.06.56
Promoted Sergeant   22.06.57
Discharged: 20.06.61
Cause of Discharge: Termination of Engagement

Service with the Colours: 26.07.51 - 09.08.53
Overseas Service; Middle East Land Force 16.11.51 - 08.02.53

Military Conduct: Very good

APPENDIX II

A SHORT HISTORY OF THE ROYAL SUSSEX REGIMENT

Origins and the 18th Century

The Regiment was raised in Belfast in 1701 by Arthur Chichester, Third Earl of Donegall, at his own expense. King William III - the former Prince of Orange - awarded the Earl's Regiment the distinction of having orange facings as a mark of his favour. In addition to being known by the successive Colonels' names, as was the custom of the time, the Regiment was also referred to as The Belfast Regiment, even when allocated the seniority number of 35th Foot in 1751.

The War of Spanish Succession 1702-1714

During the War of Spanish Succession, the 35th served on board Royal Navy warships, not as marines, but as troops who could carry out landings if need be. After taking part in the abortive attempt on Cadiz in 1702, part of the Regiment were sent to attack French and Spanish possessions in the West Indies. Disease caused heavy casualties however and by the autumn of 1703, the Regiment was back in England.

   In 1704 the Regiment was despatched to Gibraltar to reinforce the garrison during the first siege. There gaining its first battle honour Gibraltar 1704-05 in recognition for the part played in the successful defence during a major siege conducted by the French and Spanish forces. At the battle of Almanza (25th April 1707) the Regiment suffered heavy casualties, necessitating its subsequent reconstitution in Ireland.

The Seven Years War 1756-1763

1756 saw the Regiment in North America and suffering in the infamous Fort William Henry 1757 massacre at the hands of France's Indian allies, following the surrender of the fort to the French under Montcalm. Two years later after taking part in the capture of Louiseburg, the Regiment gained its major battle honour Quebec, defeating the French Royal Roussillon Regiment and avenging Fort William Henry. The storming of Martinique and Havanna in 1762 added to the Regiment's honours.

The American War of Independence 1775-1783

After serving at the battles of Bunker (Breed's) Hill 1775, Brooklyn and White Plains in 1776, the Regiment garrisoned New York. Then in 1778 it took part in the capture of St Lucia and subsequent rout of a French relieving force, returning to the West Indies in 1785.

The 19th Century
The Napoleonic Wars

The close of the 18th Century saw the Regiment, now with two battalions, serving in Flanders, distinguishing itself at Bergen op Zoom. The next major operation was the capture of Malta from the French in 1800 and immediately after this event, it was the King's Colour of the Regiment which was the first British flag to be flown from the ramparts.

The Regiment's 1st Battalion remained stationed in the Mediterranean area and played their part in General Sir John Stuart's victory over French at Maida 1806 in Italy. The hard fought but abortive invasion of Egypt followed and then the successful ejection of Napoleon's forces from the Ionian Islands and northern Italy 1809-1813.

The 2nd Battalion was with Lieutenant General Sir Charles Colville's 4th Division as right flank guard at Waterloo 1815 and took part in the Allied victory parade through Paris, before being disbanded.

The West Indies

At the close of the Napoleonic Wars, the Regiment returned once again to the West Indies until 1832. After a stay in the UK during which the title 'Royal' was bestowed on it, there followed a tour of duty in Ireland and a period of eleven years in Mauritius, where the Regiment was commended by the Governor for its good conduct.

The Indian Mutiny

In 1857 the Regiment was in Burma, but moved to Calcutta in 1857 as the Indian Mutiny flared up. After taking part in a number of operations against the mutineers, the Regiment provided an escort to the Governor General on his progress through India and were presented with new colours at Meerut. Following this, the Regiment again found itself serving in the West Indies.

107th Bengal Infantry

After the Indian Mutiny, the Regiment became linked with the 107th (Bengal Infantry) Regiment, the 107th had been raised in 1853 by the Honourable East India Company as the 3rd Bengal European Regiment, but had been transferred to the British service after the Indian Mutiny. In 1873 a common depot was established at Chichester and in 1881 the two regiments were reconstructed to form the 1st Battalion and the 2nd Battalion The Royal Sussex Regiment, 35th and 107th respectively.

Egypt 1882

The Battalion formed part of Sir Herbert Stewart's Desert Column in the vain attempt to save General Gordon in Khartoum. It fought at the battle of Abu Klea in January 1885 and helped to man the two steamers for the final attempt to reach the city. For these campaigns the Battle Honours Egypt 1882, Abu Klea and Nile 1884-5 were added to the Colours. The 2nd Battalion saw service in India during the 1891 Black Mountain Expedition and a number of punitive excursions mounted against tribesmen on the famous North West Frontier.

The Boer War

Arriving in South Africa after 'Black Week' the 1st Battalion, reinforced by the Militia and by three successive companies formed from the Regiment's Volunteer units, joined Lord Roberts' army at Bloemfontain. The Battalion took part in the successful attacks at Zand River, One Tree Hill, Diamond Hill and Ratif's Nek and in the capture of Pretoria. Subsequently the Royal Sussex formed mounted infantry columns to round up Boer commandos.

The 20th Century
The 1914-1918 War

During the First World War, the Regiment expanded to 23 Battalions. In spite of ceaseless protestations, the 1st Battalion remained in India throughout the War. The 2nd Battalion arrived in France in August 1914 as part of the 2nd Infantry Brigade, 1st Division, of the British Expeditionary Force. This Battalion was to remain in France for the four years of the War and lost 1723 officers and men killed in action during that time.

The 3rd (Militia) Battalion formed a transit depot at Newhaven; the 4th Battalion went to Gallipoli, Egypt Palestine and the Western Front; the 5th (Cinque Ports Battalion) served with the 2nd Battalion at Aubers Ridge 1915 and later went to the Italian Front. The 7th, 8th, and 9th, plus three Southdown Battalions went to France, one of the latter going to Russia after the war.

In all some 6800 members of the Regiment fell in The Great War and their names are recorded on memorial panels in the Regimental Chapel of St George in Chichester Cathedral. Four members were awarded the Victoria Cross and the Regiment received the nickname 'Iron Regiment' from their German opponents at First Ypres.

World War Two

Between the wars, the regular battalions served on the Rhine, in Ireland, Palestine, the West Indies, Malta, Chanak, Singapore and India.

In October 1940 the 1st Battalion joined the 4th Indian Division, with which it was to serve with distinction until July 1945. After seeing service in the Western Desert, the Battalion moved south to overthrow the Italians in Eritrea and Abyssinia by April 1941. Returning to the Desert the Battalion fought with distinction, particularly at Sidi Omar, November 1941 and at Wadi Akarit.

After pursing the Germans to Tunisia, the Battalion moved to Italy and fought at Cassino. In November 1944 came a move to Greece and after peace in Europe, the Battalion served in Austria, Italy once more, Palestine and Egypt. The 2nd Battalion joined the 4th and 5th in England in 133 Brigade; going to France in 1940 and being re-forming after Dunkirk. In 1942 the Brigade was sent to North Africa where it fought at Alam Haifa and El Alamein, successfully under 10th Armoured Division and 51st Highland Division during the 'break in' battles. The 4th Battalion suffered heavily when overrun by a Panzer counter attack, the ground being subsequently retaken by the 2nd Battalion. After Alamein, the 10th Parachute Battalion was formed from the 2nd Royal Sussex, one of whose members Captain Lionel Queripel, was posthumously awarded the Victoria Cross at Arnhem.

Meanwhile in Burma the 9th Battalion fought in the Arakan in early 1944, then moved to northern Burma as part of 36th Division, under command of General Stilwell's American/Chinese army. With them they drove the Japanese back to Mandalay via Mogaung, Pinure and Mongmit.

The Post War Years

In 1948 the 1st and 2nd Battalions amalgamated into the 1st Battalion. This formation served in Egypt, Jordan, Germany Korea, Gibraltar, Belfast, Malta and Aden. Whilst at home in 1963 the Battalion performed public duties in London. On 31st December 1966 the Royal Sussex Regiment became part of the newly formed Queen's Regiment.

On September 9th 1992 The Queen's Regiment amalgamated with the Royal Hampshire Regiment and became the Princess of Wales's Royal Regiment.

APPENDIX III

USEFUL ADDRESSES

The following information will be of particular interest for anyone requiring more information about the Royal Sussex Regiment or indeed wishing to join the Regimental Association.

1.   The Royal Sussex Regimental Association
Roussillon Barracks
Chichester
PO19 4BL
(01243 530852)

A Regimental Office is maintained in the Roussillon Barracks courtesy of the Corps of Royal Military Police.

The Association is still a very strong link with the Royal Sussex men and their families. It is also the Centre for all the separate Regimental associations to be found around the country.

Every year the Association organises the Annual Regimental Reunion Dinner at Lewes, The St Georges Day Service at Chichester Cathedral and the Royal Sussex Regiment Cup race at Goodwood.

The Regimental Magazine 'The Roussillon Gazette' is published once a year.

2   The Combined Services Museum
The Redoubt Fortress
Eastbourne

The Redoubt's largest collection is that of the Royal Sussex Regiment which moved to Eastbourne in 1983.

Artefacts illustrate the Regiment's service from the time it was formed in 1701. The display of medals is second to none and is superbly displayed.

The Museum Trustees are continually adding to the display either through items donated or purchased when they come up for sale.

For anybody interested in the Regiment, Militaria or just museums it is well worth visiting.

3.   West Sussex Record Office
        Chichester
        Sussex
        (01243 753600)

The Record Office houses a truly wonderful collection of document photocopies, audio-visual records and printed work appertaining to the Royal Sussex Regiment. It is recognised as being the most comprehensive of any County Regiment.

For example the photographic collection comprises nearly 7000 prints.

A very comprehensive catalogue for the Royal Sussex Collection is available which details the collection section by section.

Alan Readman, the resident archivist, with the main responsibility for the collection is an absolute mine of information regarding anything to do with the Royal Sussex.

Admittance to the Record Office is by Readers Ticket which can be obtained at the office enquiry desk.

APPENDIX IV

Home Counties Brigade.

Cinque Ports.

17th Infantry Brigade.

1st Infantry Division.

Divisional and Brigade Signs
Worn during my two years National
Service with the Royal Sussex Regt.